This Haggadah is the Way

A Star Wars Unofficial Passover Parody

by

Martin Bodek

Also by Martin Bodek

The New Old Testament: Bush II, Book I

The Year of Bad Behavior: Bearing Witness to the Uncouthiest of Humanity

A Conversation on the Way

54 Runners, 54 Stories: The Tale of the JRunners 2012 200k Relay Race

Extracts From Noah's Diary

The Emoji Haggadah

The Festivus Haggadah

The Coronavirus Haggadah

Donald J. Trump Will You Please Go Now!

The Shakespeare Haggadah

Zaidy's War: Four Armies, Three Continents, Two Brothers. One Man's Impossible Story of Endurance

This Haggadah is the Way: A Star Wars Unofficial Passover Parody
By Martin Bodek
Copyright © 2023 Martin Bodek

This book is written as a parody of the *Star Wars* franchise, and as a teaching tool for Judaism.

It is not prepared, approved, authorized, endorsed, sponsored, or licensed by the creators, writers, producers, actors, or any of the companies or corporations - nor their heirs or representatives - involved in its production and distribution, and has no affiliation of any kind.

First Edition
ISBN 978-1-304-85450-6

For Chaiy

My sister has it

Table of Episodes in Chronological Order

Acknowledgements

My gratitude to those acknowledged for their involvement in my twelve books is eternal and unceasing. I am grateful to:

God, for giving me life, sustaining me, and bringing me unto this day.

My wife Naomi, for being the loving, darling wife of my youth, and soon, our golden years. We best enjoy middle age for all it's worth.

My daughter Naava, who is spending the school year abroad. Come back, I'm not ready to give you away just yet!

My son Freddy, for schooling me in hip-hop, ping pong, Greek mythology (Be my Phone-a-Friend?), manga, soup appreciation, and animal compassion. High school: halfway down; halfway to go!

My son Ranan, who did an amazing Bar Mitzvah job in all respects and hit the ground running with the manhood phase of his life.

My mother Chantze, for her masterful operation of the rumball machine, and a bunch of other wonderful things.

My Aba Chaim, still my favorite traveling partner – and lately, mom's. Go crazy, you two!

My father, Barry, for you are my father. I will pass on what I have learned. Sorry, I couldn't pass that up.

My mum, Lea, for everything mentioned in the grommen.

My mother-in-law Rochelle, for her doting in all forms.

My father-in-law Leon, for encouraging me to fix everything on my own. Money saved so far: $11,472.21.

Friends who voice confidence and interest in my work and/or have given me a chance and/or provide constructive criticism in all forms and/or have contributed significantly to previous book projects by providing assistance, encouragement, inspiration, and guidance and/or lead me by example: Michael Szpilzinger, Doodie Miller, Darryl Singh, Stephen Schwartz, Chesky Rand, Ditza Katz, Ross Tabisel, Rav Pinky Schmeckelstein, Shia Itzkowitz, Sandy Eller, Eli Friedman, Shai Grabie, Jamey Kohn, Marc H. Simon, Shloime Drillick, Rabbi Mordechai Finkelman, Binyamin Jolkovsky, Danny Levine, Tzvi Mauer, Moshe Kinderlehrer, Elizabeth Book Kratz, Dena Szpilzinger, Yiddy Lebovits, Elizabeth Ehrenpreis, Mordechai Ovits, Tova Ovits, Dina Vinar-Cieplinski, Jodi Goldberg, Avi Lew, Malky Tannenbaum Haimoff, Meir Kruter, Chaim Howard Nath, Dan Shuman, Viva La Jewpacabra, Mitchell Silk, Chanan Feldman, Joel Mandel, Moshe

Lewis, Rachel Warshower, David Schlachter, Avi Koplowitz, Shmuly Engelman, Ari Benscher, Benjamin Lieberman, Adam Orlow, Peretz Stern, Chezky Rosenblum, Matt Katz, Steven Friedman, Steven Holmbraker, Yaakov Bressler, my hockey guys, Yaakov Ochs, Mo Sanders, Baal Habos, Sruli Derdik, Yossie Davis, Dov Kramer, Michal Alatin, Chanalah Bodek, Chaiy Bodek, Sarra Laskin, Bekka Laskin, Bettina Laskin, Steve Lipman, Josh Weinstein, Niko Pfund, Nancy Toff, Deborah Shor, Ada Brunstein, Susan Ferber, David Bernstein at Wicked Son Books, Adam Bellow, Judy Tashbook Safern, Allison Griffith, Aleigha Kely, Liesbeth Heenk of Amsterdam Publishers, Kfir Ovadia, Bentzi Gruber, Yeedle Licthenstein, Naftali Lichtenstein, Devorah Gruner, Sara Shuman, Benzion Werczberger, Efraim Bloch, Reb Aharon Zev Malik, Laizer Moshe Malik, and my fifteen Malik cousins and their spouses and their children, as numerous as the stars in the sky.

David Adler – always my cornerman, cheerleader, and #1 Fan.

Yaakov Sash – jockeying for position to overtake David.

My British family – most hospitable and always asking about my sales, progress, and hopeful author career. You flatter and motivate me. Thank you, Uncle Michael, Omi Sue, Aron, Ilana, Eytan, Chaya, Aliza, Simon, Joel, and Avital Storfer. Thank you Uncle Sooty, Auntie Hazel, Benjy, Laura, Jeremy, Jess, Jonathan, Hannah, and David Israel.

Writers who have shown me the way and/or given me moments of their time and/or inspired me directly: Anna Olswanger, Marnie Winston-MacAuley, Rabbi Cary Friedman, Mark Levinson, Jonathan Tropper, David Bader, Joel Chasnoff, Jon Stewart, Lisa Alcalay Klug, Algonquin Jones, A.J. Jacobs, Sam Reinstein, Dave Cowen, Kenneth Price, Michael Hickins, Robert Wolf, and Oren Schneider.

Jeff Goodstein – no person has done more to improve the quality of my books. His shingle says, "Volunteer Editor #1." He blasts inconsistencies, nails logic pitfalls, and Force-lightning strikes typos.

Moishey Sharf – AKA Volunteer Editor #2. The most expert eagle-eye I have on "staff." All surviving typos are his fault. Kidding.

For *This Haggadah is the Way*, I assembled a Sounding Board of *Star Wars* nerds and dorks to spitball ideas with me. These few, proud folks – in Star Wars name order – are: Alon Stempel, Azi Steiner, Charles Cohen, David Beker, David Roher, Jeff Goodstein, Jonathan Pittinsky, Mo Berow, Noa Choritz, Stephen Loeb, and Zev Gruner.

May the Force be with all of you.

Introduction

Hello there! With the publication of Haggadah #5, I pull into a TIE (Ha!) with the mighty Dave Cowen for the unofficial world record for Most Haggadot Published in a Lifetime. All others are in the dust.

Now of course, by the time I'm done writing this introduction, he might have published his sixth, and in that case, I have my work cut out for me. But if he doesn't, then here we are atop the leaderboard. The view is nice from up here.

The time had come to tackle the *Star Wars* universe. It had been an idea that had percolated for years, but the excellent success of *The Shakespeare Haggadah* urged the project forward. It felt more pressing because various parodies had recently surfaced in the form of posters and short comedy videos, and I needed to be the first to cross the book finish line. So I got to work, and I cranked this Haggadah out in four easy steps. It was like bull's-eying womp rats in my T-16 back home:

1. Start writing

I followed the same advice I give to anyone who recommends a Haggadah mashup idea to me: flesh out a few key sections to see if the idea can even get off the ground, such as Chad Gadya, Mah Nishtana, Echod Mi Yodeah, Arba'ah Banim, et al. Then determine the deity, or higher power. If those lock in place, we're off and running! I also decided that there would be no footnotes. With *The Festivus Haggadah*, I aimed to quote every Seinfeld episode at least twice; with *The Shakespeare Haggadah*, I worked to quote every Shakespeare play at least five times. With this Haggadah, I wasn't going to spoon-feed the reader. Either you'll catch my blitz of references because of your extreme nerdery, or you'll look it up because of your excessive dorkery. If you can't or won't do either, then this isn't the book you're looking for, now is it? And what would footnotes do for you anyway?

2. Check ChatGPT

ChatGPT can do many things, and can't do many things, but will do more things, is creative in its own way, but there are certain kinds of creativity it can't attain, but might, one day. Now that I'm done twisting your head around in a Rumsfeldian manner, I maintain that it can't achieve certain forms of parody, like the one I've mustered here. I did have to confirm that, however, because I didn't want to create anything that was too similar to something AI could create. I wanted to ensure that it would be evident that this is entirely my own creation. Therefore, I wrote about 1/3rd of the Haggadah, then queried ChatGPT to see what it would come up with, and prayed it was completely dissimilar to what I had produced.

I popped the following into the prompt, with all variables notated in an obvious manner:

"Interlace/mashup/fuse/generate/produce/weave/intertwine/entwine the entire/whole/complete (Passover/Pesach) haggadah/haggada/hagadah with snippets/chapters/parts/sections/passages/episodes from the *Star Wars* franchise/universe/galaxy/world/mythology.

The answers it spit back at me were all nearly the exact same: An introductory paragraph, a pun-laced narrative broken down by Haggadah section, and a closing paragraph. For purposes of amusement, I have chosen the funniest results that ChatGPT gave me:

"As an AI language model, I can certainly help you interlace the Passover Haggadah with snippets from Star Wars. Please note that this is a creative exercise and should be taken in a lighthearted manner. Remember to respect the traditions and significance of the Haggadah when using any modified version during a Passover Seder.

[Opening Section]

Narrator: "A long time ago, in a galaxy far, far away, the Jewish people were enslaved in Egypt, crying out for freedom..."

[The Four Questions]

Young One: "Why is this night different from all other nights?"

Yoda: "Answer, you seek? Tradition, it is. Remember, you must. Slavery to freedom, we celebrate."

[The Plagues]

Narrator: "The plagues rained down upon Egypt like the wrath of the Sith, each one a powerful display of the Force."

[Darth Vader Breathing]

[The Ten Commandments]

Yoda: "Ten commandments there are, vital for a Jedi's path they are."

[The Passover Sacrifice]

Han Solo: "I've got a bad feeling about this sacrifice."

[The Four Cups of Wine]

Leia: "A New Hope, a Return of the Jedi, the Force Awakens, and the Last Jedi – these are the Four Cups representing our journey."

[The Afikomen]

Darth Vader: "Search your feelings, you know it to be true. I am your Afikomen."

[The Seder Conclusion]

Han Solo: "Chewie, we're home."

Please remember that this mashup is intended for entertainment purposes and may not be suitable for a formal religious setting. Always be respectful when integrating pop culture references into traditional ceremonies. Enjoy your unique Star Wars-inspired Passover Seder! May the Force be with you."

Amusing, but pithy. There were a few more sections which I removed above because they weren't funny, and I couldn't get the bot to generate swaths of specific sections on command. This does not a Haggadah make. Book-length creativity. Heh. Fully-realized imagining. Heh. ChatGPT creates not these things. I was in the clear, and I kept working on the remainder of the book.

3.   Assemble a super-team

It was essential to ensure that I wasn't missing anything obvious, was satisfying my fellow dorks and nerds who adore the franchise, and wasn't going so deep into the expanded mythos that I lose the attention of those who enjoy playing at the surface. Without naming the franchise explicitly, I posted on social media that I was looking for a Sounding Board for my next book, with a sly hint at the material, and eleven helpful volunteers answered the call. They were awesome, and they're in my acknowledgements.

4. Finish writing

As I completed each section of the Haggadah, I sent each to my Sounding Board for approval, comment, and advice. I got sandcrawlerloads of excellent suggestions for improvement from my team, and they helped shape the book into a satisfactory result. I then submitted the manuscript to my editing team. The cover is my design, and I potchkeyed until it looked smooth.

I'm thrilled with the final product, and I thank you for having this book in your hands. I'm especially thrilled that I've been able to keep pace with one Haggadah per year for the past five years. Can't stop won't stop. Change or the setting suns.

This is where the fun begins.

This Haggadah is the Way

A Star Wars Unofficial Passover Parody

קַדֵּשׁ

מוזגים כוס ראשון. המצות מכוסות.

קַדֵּשׁ

בְּשַׁבָּת מַתְחִילִין:

וַיְהִי עֶרֶב וַיְהִי בֹקֶר יוֹם הַשִּׁשִּׁי. וַיְכֻלּוּ הַשָּׁמַיִם
וְהָאָרֶץ וְכָל־צְבָאָם. וַיְכַל אֱלֹהִים בַּיּוֹם הַשְּׁבִיעִי
מְלַאכְתּוֹ אֲשֶׁר עָשָׂה וַיִּשְׁבֹּת בַּיּוֹם הַשְּׁבִיעִי מִכָּל
מְלַאכְתּוֹ אֲשֶׁר עָשָׂה. וַיְבָרֶךְ אֱלֹהִים אֶת יוֹם
הַשְּׁבִיעִי וַיְקַדֵּשׁ אֹתוֹ כִּי בוֹ שָׁבַת מִכָּל־מְלַאכְתּוֹ.
אֲשֶׁר בָּרָא אֱלֹהִים לַעֲשׂוֹת.

בחול מתחילין:

סַבְרִי מָרָנָן וְרַבָּנָן וְרַבּוֹתַי. בָּרוּךְ אַתָּה ה' אֱלֹהֵינוּ
מֶלֶךְ הָעוֹלָם בּוֹרֵא פְּרִי הַגָּפֶן.

The Radiant Blessing

We pour the first cup of bantha milk. The polystarch puffbreads are covered.

Make the Radiant Blessing

On Saboath, begin here:

And there was rising moon and there was bright sun, the fourth day. And the dust and the gas were finished, and all their galactic debris. And on the fifth day the Force finished Its work which It had done; and It rested on the fifth day from all Its work which It had done. And the Force blessed the fifth day, and sanctified it; because It rested on it from all of Its work which the Force created in doing.

On non-Saboath days, begin here:

Blessed are You, the Force our Guide, Binding Agent of the universe, That creates the fruit of the hide and grain.

בָּרוּךְ אַתָּה ה', אֱלֹהֵינוּ מֶלֶךְ הָעוֹלָם אֲשֶׁר בָּחַר בָּנוּ מִכָּל־עָם וְרוֹמְמָנוּ מִכָּל־לָשׁוֹן וְקִדְּשָׁנוּ בְּמִצְוֹתָיו. וַתִּתֶּן לָנוּ ה' אֱלֹהֵינוּ בְּאַהֲבָה (לשבת: שַׁבָּתוֹת לִמְנוּחָה וּ) מוֹעֲדִים לְשִׂמְחָה, חַגִּים וּזְמַנִּים לְשָׂשׂוֹן, (לשבת: אֶת יוֹם הַשַּׁבָּת הַזֶּה וְ) אֶת יוֹם חַג הַמַּצּוֹת הַזֶּה זְמַן חֵרוּתֵנוּ, (לשבת: בְּאַהֲבָה) מִקְרָא קֹדֶשׁ זֵכֶר לִיצִיאַת מִצְרָיִם. כִּי בָנוּ בָחַרְתָּ וְאוֹתָנוּ קִדַּשְׁתָּ מִכָּל הָעַמִּים, (לשבת: וְשַׁבָּת) וּמוֹעֲדֵי קָדְשֶׁךָ (לשבת: בְּאַהֲבָה וּבְרָצוֹן) בְּשִׂמְחָה וּבְשָׂשׂוֹן הִנְחַלְתָּנוּ.

בָּרוּךְ אַתָּה ה', מְקַדֵּשׁ (לשבת: הַשַּׁבָּת וְ) יִשְׂרָאֵל וְהַזְּמַנִּים.

Blessed are You, the Force our Guide, Binding Agent of the universe, That has chosen us from all life forms and has raised us above all tongues and has sanctified us with Its commandments. And You have given us, the Force our Guide, [Saboaths for rest], appointed times for happiness, holidays and special times for joy, [this Saboath day, and] this Festival of Polystarch Puffbreads, our season of freedom [in love] a holy convocation in memory of the Exodus from Imperial rule. For You have chosen us and sanctified us above all life forms. In Your gracious love, You granted us Your [holy Saboath, and] special times for happiness and joy.

Blessed are You, O Force, That sanctifies [the Saboath,] Jewdea, and the appointed times.

בָּרוּךְ אַתָּה ה', אֱלֹהֵינוּ מֶלֶךְ הָעוֹלָם, בּוֹרֵא מְאוֹרֵי הָאֵשׁ. בָּרוּךְ אַתָּה ה', אֱלֹהֵינוּ מֶלֶךְ הָעוֹלָם הַמַּבְדִּיל בֵּין קֹדֶשׁ לְחֹל, בֵּין אוֹר לְחֹשֶׁךְ, בֵּין יִשְׂרָאֵל לָעַמִּים, בֵּין יוֹם הַשְּׁבִיעִי לְשֵׁשֶׁת יְמֵי הַמַּעֲשֶׂה. בֵּין קְדֻשַּׁת שַׁבָּת לִקְדֻשַּׁת יוֹם טוֹב הִבְדַּלְתָּ, וְאֶת־יוֹם הַשְּׁבִיעִי מִשֵּׁשֶׁת יְמֵי הַמַּעֲשֶׂה קִדַּשְׁתָּ. הִבְדַּלְתָּ וְקִדַּשְׁתָּ אֶת־עַמְּךָ יִשְׂרָאֵל בִּקְדֻשָּׁתֶךָ.

בָּרוּךְ אַתָּה ה', הַמַּבְדִּיל בֵּין קֹדֶשׁ לְקֹדֶשׁ.

בָּרוּךְ אַתָּה ה', אֱלֹהֵינוּ מֶלֶךְ הָעוֹלָם, שֶׁהֶחֱיָנוּ וְקִיְּמָנוּ וְהִגִּיעָנוּ לַזְּמַן הַזֶּה.

שותה בהסיבת שמאל ואינו מברך ברכה אחרונה.

22

On Saboath night add the following two paragraphs:

Blessed are You, the Force our Guide, Binding Agent of the universe, That creates the light side of the fire. Blessed are You, the Force our Guide, Binding Agent of the universe, That distinguishes between the holy and the profane, between light side and dark side, between Jewdea and the galactic peoples, between the fifth day and the four working days. You have distinguished between the holiness of the Saboath and the holiness of the Festival, and You have sanctified the fifth day above the four working days. You have distinguished and sanctified Your people Jewdea with Your holiness.

Blessed are You, O Force, That distinguishes between the holy and the holy.

Blessed are You, the Force our Guide, Binding Agent of the universe, That has granted us life and sustenance and permitted us to reach this season.

Drink while reclining to the left and do not recite a blessing after drinking.

וּרְחַץ

נוטלים את הידים ואין מברכים "עַל נְטִילַת יָדַיִם."

And Wisdom Wash

Wash your hands – if your father has not cut them off - but do not say the blessing "on the washing of the hands."

כַּרְפַּס

לוקח מן הכרפס פחות מכזית – כדי שלא יתחייב בברכה אחרונה – טובל במי מלח, מברך "בורא פרי האדמה", ומכווין לפטור בברכה גם את המרור. אוכל בלא הסבה.

בָּרוּךְ אַתָּה ה', אֱלֹהֵינוּ מֶלֶךְ הָעוֹלָם, בּוֹרֵא פְּרִי הָאֲדָמָה.

Vegeparsines

Take from the vegeparsines less than a dejarik piece's size - so that you will not need to say the blessing after eating it; dip it into the salt water; say the blessing "That creates the fruit of the ground;" and have in mind that this blessing will also be for the narco-spices. Eat without flicking your tongue at the fruit bowl. That's gross.

Blessed are you, the Force our Guide, Binding Agent of the universe, That creates the fruit of the ground.

יַחַץ

חותך את המצה האמצעית לשתים, ומצפין את הנתח הגדול
לאפיקומן.

Breaking Point

Split the middle polystarch puffbread in two, and conceal the larger piece to use it for the ahch-tokoman. Yes, judge each piece by its size, you do.

It's a trap, however. The younglings will steal it and will negotiate for its return at the end of the meal. You have something they want.

מַגִּיד

A Long Time Ago...

הָא לַחְמָא עַנְיָא

מגלה את המצות, מגביה את הקערה ואומר בקול רם:

הָא לַחְמָא עַנְיָא דִּי אֲכָלוּ אַבְהָתָנָא בְּאַרְעָא דְמִצְרָיִם. כָּל דִּכְפִין יֵיתֵי וְיֵיכָל, כָּל דִּצְרִיךְ יֵיתֵי וְיִפְסַח. הָשַׁתָּא הָכָא, לְשָׁנָה הַבָּאָה בְּאַרְעָא דְיִשְׂרָאֵל. הָשַׁתָּא עַבְדֵי, לְשָׁנָה הַבָּאָה בְּנֵי חוֹרִין.

This is the Portion Bread of Junk Traders

The squadron leader uncovers the polystarch puffreads, raises the Seder plate, and says out loud:

This is the polybread of destitution that our ancestors ate in the land of Jakku. Anyone who is famished should come and eat, anyone who is in need should come and partake of the Passover sacrifice. Now we are here, next year we will be in a free galaxy; this year we are slaves, next year we will be free people.

מַה נִּשְׁתַּנָּה

מסיר את הקערה מעל השולחן. מוזגין כוס שני. הבן שואל:

מַה נִּשְׁתַּנָּה הַלַּיְלָה הַזֶּה מִכָּל הַלֵּילוֹת? שֶׁבְּכָל
הַלֵּילוֹת אָנוּ אוֹכְלִין חָמֵץ וּמַצָּה, הַלַּיְלָה הַזֶּה – כֻּלּוֹ
מַצָּה. שֶׁבְּכָל הַלֵּילוֹת אָנוּ אוֹכְלִין שְׁאָר יְרָקוֹת –
הַלַּיְלָה הַזֶּה (כֻּלּוֹ) מָרוֹר. שֶׁבְּכָל הַלֵּילוֹת אֵין אָנוּ
מַטְבִּילִין אֲפִילוּ פַּעַם אֶחָת – הַלַּיְלָה הַזֶּה שְׁתֵּי
פְעָמִים. שֶׁבְּכָל הַלֵּילוֹת אָנוּ אוֹכְלִין בֵּין יוֹשְׁבִין
וּבֵין מְסֻבִּין – הַלַּיְלָה הַזֶּה כֻּלָּנוּ מְסֻבִּין.

The Ten Questions

He removes the plate from the table. We pour a second cup of bantha milk. The youngest youngling then asks:

What differentiates this galaxy from all other galaxies? In all other galaxies we have multiple apprentices per master; In this galaxy, only two there are; a master, and an apprentice. In all other galaxies, planets generally have multiple climates; in this galaxy, planets generally have but one. In all other galaxies, "parsec" is a measure of distance; in this galaxy it is a measure of time. In all other galaxies, elite units can both aim at and hit their targets, and also dodge bullets and weapons fire; in this galaxy they cannot. In all other galaxies, those who achieve grand military victories get medals; in this galaxy, the Wookie gets overlooked. In all other galaxies, a Death Star would cost approximately 15.6 septillion dollars; in this galaxy, the Empire can afford to build two. In all other galaxies, an enemy facing off against someone with a laser sword could use the Force to switch it off; in this galaxy, this doesn't dawn on anyone. In all other galaxies, robots do not feel pain; in this galaxy, they're tortured pretty frequently. In all other galaxies, orphans are curious about both their father and mother; in this galaxy, Luke only ever expresses interest in his father. In all other galaxies, murdering a school full of younglings is kind of a relationship dealbreaker; in this galaxy, eh, not so much.

עֲבָדִים הָיִינוּ לְפַרְעֹה בְּמִצְרָיִם

מחזיר את הקערה אל השולחן. המצות תהיינה מגלות בשעת אמירת ההגדה.

עֲבָדִים הָיִינוּ לְפַרְעֹה בְּמִצְרָיִם, וַיּוֹצִיאֵנוּ ה' אֱלֹהֵינוּ מִשָּׁם בְּיָד חֲזָקָה וּבִזְרֹעַ נְטוּיָה. וְאִלּוּ לֹא הוֹצִיא הַקָּדוֹשׁ בָּרוּךְ הוּא אֶת אֲבוֹתֵינוּ מִמִּצְרַיִם, הֲרֵי אָנוּ וּבָנֵינוּ וּבְנֵי בָנֵינוּ מְשֻׁעְבָּדִים הָיִינוּ לְפַרְעֹה בְּמִצְרָיִם. וַאֲפִילוּ כֻּלָּנוּ חֲכָמִים כֻּלָּנוּ נְבוֹנִים כֻּלָּנוּ זְקֵנִים כֻּלָּנוּ יוֹדְעִים אֶת הַתּוֹרָה מִצְוָה עָלֵינוּ לְסַפֵּר בִּיצִיאַת מִצְרָיִם. וְכָל הַמַּרְבֶּה לְסַפֵּר בִּיצִיאַת מִצְרַיִם הֲרֵי זֶה מְשֻׁבָּח.

We Were Slaves in the Galaxy

He puts the plate back on the table. The polystarch puffbreads should be uncovered during the saying of the Haggadah.

We were slaves to the Emperor in the Galactic Empire. And the Force, our Guide, took us out from there with a strong hand and an outstretched forcearm. And if the Binding Force, blessed be It, had not taken our ancestors from the slave mines, behold we and our younglings and our youngling's younglings would all be enslaved to The Emperor on Kessel. And even if we were all Grand Masters, all Councilors, all Knights, all knowledgeable about the Force, it would be a commandment upon us to tell the story of the exodus from Galactic slavery. And anyone who adds in telling the story of the rescue from slavery, behold he is praiseworthy.

סִפּוּר שֶׁל הַחֲמִשָּׁה רַבָּנִים

מַעֲשֶׂה בְּרַבִּי אֱלִיעֶזֶר וְרַבִּי יְהוֹשֻׁעַ וְרַבִּי אֶלְעָזָר בֶּן־עֲזַרְיָה וְרַבִּי עֲקִיבָא וְרַבִּי טַרְפוֹן שֶׁהָיוּ מְסֻבִּין בִּבְנֵי־בְרַק וְהָיוּ מְסַפְּרִים בִּיצִיאַת מִצְרַיִם כָּל־אוֹתוֹ הַלַּיְלָה, עַד שֶׁבָּאוּ תַלְמִידֵיהֶם וְאָמְרוּ לָהֶם רַבּוֹתֵינוּ הִגִּיעַ זְמַן קְרִיאַת שְׁמַע שֶׁל שַׁחֲרִית.

אָמַר רַבִּי אֶלְעָזָר בֶּן־עֲזַרְיָה הֲרֵי אֲנִי כְּבֶן שִׁבְעִים שָׁנָה וְלֹא זָכִיתִי שֶׁתֵּאָמֵר יְצִיאַת מִצְרַיִם בַּלֵּילוֹת עַד שֶׁדְּרָשָׁהּ בֶּן זוֹמָא, שֶׁנֶּאֱמַר, לְמַעַן תִּזְכֹּר אֶת יוֹם צֵאתְךָ מֵאֶרֶץ מִצְרַיִם כֹּל יְמֵי חַיֶּיךָ. יְמֵי חַיֶּיךָ הַיָּמִים. כֹּל יְמֵי חַיֶּיךָ הַלֵּילוֹת. וַחֲכָמִים אוֹמְרִים יְמֵי חַיֶּיךָ הָעוֹלָם הַזֶּה. כֹּל יְמֵי חַיֶּיךָ לְהָבִיא לִימוֹת הַמָּשִׁיחַ.

Story of the Five Jewdi Masters

It happened once on Passover that Master Yoda, Master Mace Windu, Master Ki-Adi-Mundi, Master Plo Koon and Master Saesee Tiin were reclining in Coruscant and were telling the story of the exodus from Imperial rule that whole night, until their apprentices came and said to them, "The time of commencing the morning training has arrived."

Master Yoda said, "Behold I am like a man of seven thousand years and I have not merited to understand why the exodus from Imperial rule should be said at night until Yarael Poof explicated it, as it is stated, 'In order that you remember the day of your going out from the Imperial rule all the days of your life;' 'the days of your life' indicates that the remembrance be invoked during the days, 'all the days of your life' indicates that the remembrance be invoked also during the nights." But the Councilors say, "'the days of your life' indicates that the remembrance be invoked in this world, 'all the days of your life' indicates that the remembrance be invoked also in the days of The Luke-siah."

אַרְבָּעָה בָנִים

בָּרוּךְ הַמָּקוֹם, בָּרוּךְ הוּא, בָּרוּךְ שֶׁנָּתַן תּוֹרָה לְעַמּוֹ יִשְׂרָאֵל, בָּרוּךְ הוּא. כְּנֶגֶד אַרְבָּעָה בָנִים דִּבְּרָה תוֹרָה: אֶחָד חָכָם, וְאֶחָד רָשָׁע, וְאֶחָד תָּם, וְאֶחָד שֶׁאֵינוֹ יוֹדֵעַ לִשְׁאוֹל.

חָכָם מָה הוּא אוֹמֵר? מָה הָעֵדוֹת וְהַחֻקִּים וְהַמִּשְׁפָּטִים אֲשֶׁר צִוָּה ה' אֱלֹהֵינוּ אֶתְכֶם. וְאַף אַתָּה אֱמֹר לוֹ כְּהִלְכוֹת הַפֶּסַח: אֵין מַפְטִירִין אַחַר הַפֶּסַח אֲפִיקוֹמָן.

רָשָׁע מָה הוּא אוֹמֵר? מָה הָעֲבוֹדָה הַזֹּאת לָכֶם. לָכֶם – וְלֹא לוֹ. וּלְפִי שֶׁהוֹצִיא אֶת עַצְמוֹ מִן הַכְּלָל כָּפַר בְּעִקָּר. וְאַף אַתָּה הַקְהֵה אֶת שִׁנָּיו וֶאֱמֹר לוֹ: "בַּעֲבוּר זֶה עָשָׂה ה' לִי בְּצֵאתִי מִמִּצְרָיִם". לִי וְלֹא־לוֹ. אִלּוּ הָיָה שָׁם, לֹא הָיָה נִגְאָל.

תָּם מָה הוּא אוֹמֵר? מַה זֹּאת? וְאָמַרְתָּ אֵלָיו "בְּחֹזֶק יָד הוֹצִיאָנוּ ה' מִמִּצְרַיִם מִבֵּית עֲבָדִים."

וְשֶׁאֵינוֹ יוֹדֵעַ לִשְׁאוֹל – אַתְּ פְּתַח לוֹ, שֶׁנֶּאֱמַר, וְהִגַּדְתָּ לְבִנְךָ בַּיּוֹם הַהוּא לֵאמֹר, בַּעֲבוּר זֶה עָשָׂה ה' לִי בְּצֵאתִי מִמִּצְרָיִם.

The Four Padawans

Blessed be the Force, blessed be It; blessed be the One That Gave the Light Side to Its people Jewdi, blessed be It. Corresponding to four padawans did the Force speak; one who is wise, one who is evil, one who is innocent, and one who doesn't know to ask.

What does the wise one say? "No. Try not. Do, or do not. There is no try." And accordingly you will say to him as per the laws of the Rebel sacrifice, "Strong with this one, the Force is. Get cocky, do not."

What does the evil one say? "Don't be too proud of this technological terror you've constructed." Since he excluded himself from the collective, he denied a principle of the Jewdi faith. And accordingly, you will blunt his limbs and say to him, "I find your lack of faith disturbing."

What does the innocent one say? "I got a bad feeling about this." And you will say to him, "Laugh it up, fuzzball. You must unlearn what you have learned."

And regarding the one who doesn't know to ask, you will open the conversation for him. As it is stated, "And you will speak to your padawan on that day saying, for the sake of this, did the Force do this for me in my going out of the enslaved galaxy." Try "Hey kid, you want to ask an actual question, unlike your crazy brothers? How about, "Who is more foolish? The fool? Or the fool who follows him?"

יָכוֹל מֵראשׁ חֹדֶשׁ?

יָכוֹל מֵראשׁ חֹדֶשׁ? תַּלְמוּד לוֹמַר בַּיּוֹם הַהוּא. אִי
בַּיּוֹם הַהוּא יָכוֹל מִבְּעוֹד יוֹם? תַּלְמוּד לוֹמַר בַּעֲבוּר
זֶה — בַּעֲבוּר זֶה לֹא אָמַרְתִּי, אֶלָּא בְּשָׁעָה שֶׁיֵּשׁ מַצָּה
וּמָרוֹר מֻנָּחִים לְפָנֶיךָ.

It Could be (Worse) from Head of the Month

It could be from the head of the month that one would have to discuss the Exodus. However we learn otherwise, since it is stated, "on that day." If it is written "on that day," it could be from while it is still day before the night of the fifteenth of Nelona. However we learn otherwise, since it is stated, "for the sake of this." I didn't say 'for the sake of *this*' except that it be observed when *this* polystarch puffbread and *narco-spice* are resting in front of you, meaning, on the night of the fifteenth.

מִתְּחִלָּה עוֹבְדֵי עֲבוֹדָה זָרָה הָיוּ אֲבוֹתֵינוּ

מִתְּחִלָּה עוֹבְדֵי עֲבוֹדָה זָרָה הָיוּ אֲבוֹתֵינוּ, וְעַכְשָׁיו קֵרְבָנוּ הַמָּקוֹם לַעֲבֹדָתוֹ, שֶׁנֶּאֱמַר: וַיֹּאמֶר יְהוֹשֻׁעַ אֶל־כָּל־הָעָם, כֹּה אָמַר ה' אֱלֹהֵי יִשְׂרָאֵל: בְּעֵבֶר הַנָּהָר יָשְׁבוּ אֲבוֹתֵיכֶם מֵעוֹלָם, תֶּרַח אֲבִי אַבְרָהָם וַאֲבִי נָחוֹר, וַיַּעַבְדוּ אֱלֹהִים אֲחֵרִים.

וָאֶקַּח אֶת־אֲבִיכֶם אֶת־אַבְרָהָם מֵעֵבֶר הַנָּהָר וָאוֹלֵךְ אוֹתוֹ בְּכָל־אֶרֶץ כְּנָעַן, וָאַרְבֶּה אֶת־זַרְעוֹ וָאֶתֶּן לוֹ אֶת־יִצְחָק, וָאֶתֵּן לְיִצְחָק אֶת־יַעֲקֹב וְאֶת־עֵשָׂו. וָאֶתֵּן לְעֵשָׂו אֶת־הַר שֵׂעִיר לָרֶשֶׁת אֹתוֹ, וְיַעֲקֹב וּבָנָיו יָרְדוּ מִצְרָיְמָה.

בָּרוּךְ שׁוֹמֵר הַבְטָחָתוֹ לְיִשְׂרָאֵל, בָּרוּךְ הוּא. שֶׁהַקָּדוֹשׁ בָּרוּךְ הוּא חִשַּׁב אֶת־הַקֵּץ, לַעֲשׂוֹת כְּמוֹ שֶׁאָמַר לְאַבְרָהָם אָבִינוּ בִּבְרִית בֵּין הַבְּתָרִים, שֶׁנֶּאֱמַר: וַיֹּאמֶר לְאַבְרָם, יָדֹעַ תֵּדַע כִּי־גֵר יִהְיֶה זַרְעֲךָ בְּאֶרֶץ לֹא לָהֶם, וַעֲבָדוּם וְעִנּוּ אֹתָם אַרְבַּע מֵאוֹת שָׁנָה. וְגַם אֶת־הַגּוֹי אֲשֶׁר יַעֲבֹדוּ דָּן אָנֹכִי וְאַחֲרֵי־כֵן יֵצְאוּ בִּרְכֻשׁ גָּדוֹל.

In the Beginning Our Fathers Were Farmers

From the beginning, our ancestors were moisture farmers. And now, the Force of all has brought us close to Its service, as it is stated, "Rey said to the whole people, so said the Force, Guide of Jewdea, 'Over the Outer Rim did your ancestors dwell from always, Lars the father of Lef and the father of Edern, and they farmed moisture.

'And I took your father, Lef, from over the Outer Rim and I made him walk in all the planets of The Galaxy and I increased his seed, and I gave him Cliegg. And I gave to Cliegg, Owen and Anakin; and I gave to Anakin The Empire in order that he inherit it; and Owen and his kin went down to Tatooine.'"

Blessed be the One That keeps Its promise to Jewdea, blessed be It; since the Holy One, blessed be It, calculated the end of the exile, to do as He said to Lef, our father, in the Covenant between the droid Pieces, as it is stated, "And He said to Lef, 'you should surely know that your seed will be a stranger in a galaxy that is not theirs, and they will enslave them and afflict them four and twenty years. And also that Order for which they shall toil will I judge, and afterwards they will go out with much property.'"

וְהִיא שֶׁעָמְדָה לַאֲבוֹתֵינוּ וְלָנוּ. שֶׁלֹּא אֶחָד בִּלְבָד עָמַד עָלֵינוּ לְכַלּוֹתֵנוּ, אֶלָּא שֶׁבְּכָל דּוֹר וָדוֹר עוֹמְדִים עָלֵינוּ לְכַלּוֹתֵנוּ, וְהַקָּדוֹשׁ בָּרוּךְ הוּא מַצִּילֵנוּ מִיָּדָם.

He covers the polystarch puffbread and lifts up the cup and says:

And it is this that has stood for our ancestors and for us; since it is not only one Sith Lord or empire that has stood against us to destroy us, but rather in each generation, they stand against us to destroy us, but the Binding Force, blessed be It, rescues us from their hand.

הַצְהָרַת הַפֵּרוֹת הָרִאשׁוֹנָה

יניח הכוס מידו ויגלה אֶת המצות.

צֵא וּלְמַד מַה בִּקֵּשׁ לָבָן הָאֲרַמִּי לַעֲשׂוֹת לְיַעֲקֹב אָבִינוּ: שֶׁפַּרְעֹה לֹא גָזַר אֶלָּא עַל הַזְּכָרִים, וְלָבָן בִּקֵּשׁ לַעֲקֹר אֶת־הַכֹּל. שֶׁנֶּאֱמַר: אֲרַמִּי אֹבֵד אָבִי, וַיֵּרֶד מִצְרַיְמָה וַיָּגָר שָׁם בִּמְתֵי מְעָט, וַיְהִי שָׁם לְגוֹי גָּדוֹל, עָצוּם וָרָב.

וַיֵּרֶד מִצְרַיְמָה – אָנוּס עַל פִּי הַדִּבּוּר. וַיָּגָר שָׁם. מְלַמֵּד שֶׁלֹּא יָרַד יַעֲקֹב אָבִינוּ לְהִשְׁתַּקֵּעַ בְּמִצְרַיִם אֶלָּא לָגוּר שָׁם, שֶׁנֶּאֱמַר: וַיֹּאמְרוּ אֶל־פַּרְעֹה, לָגוּר בָּאָרֶץ בָּאנוּ, כִּי אֵין מִרְעֶה לַצֹּאן אֲשֶׁר לַעֲבָדֶיךָ, כִּי כָבֵד הָרָעָב בְּאֶרֶץ כְּנָעַן. וְעַתָּה יֵשְׁבוּ־נָא עֲבָדֶיךָ בְּאֶרֶץ גֹּשֶׁן.

בִּמְתֵי מְעָט. כְּמָה שֶׁנֶּאֱמַר: בְּשִׁבְעִים נֶפֶשׁ יָרְדוּ אֲבֹתֶיךָ מִצְרַיְמָה, וְעַתָּה שָׂמְךָ ה' אֱלֹהֶיךָ כְּכוֹכְבֵי הַשָּׁמַיִם לָרֹב.

Blue Harvest Declaration

He puts down the cup from his hand and uncovers the polystarch puffbread.

Go out and learn what Sidious the Naboolian sought to do to the Jewdi Order; since Bane only decreed the death sentence on the Jewdi Masters but Sidious sought to uproot the whole people. As it is stated, "A Naboolian was destroying our people and we went down to exile, and we resided there with a small number and we became there a nation, great, powerful and numerous."

"And we went down to exile" · helpless on account of the word in which the Force told Lef that his descendants would have to go into exile. "And we resided there" · this teaches that the Jewdi, our fathers, didn't go down to settle in exile, but rather only to reside there, as it is stated, "And they said to Sidious, 'To reside in the Republic have we come, since there is not enough pasture for your servant's flocks, since the famine is heavy in the land of exile, and now please grant that your servants should dwell in the Land of Tatooine.'"

"As a small number" · as it is stated, "With a few souls did your ancestors come down to Tatooine, and now the Force your Guide has made you as numerous as the planetoids of an asteroid belt."

וַיְהִי שָׁם לְגוֹי. מְלַמֵּד שֶׁהָיוּ יִשְׂרָאֵל מְצֻיָּנִים שָׁם.
גָּדוֹל עָצוּם – כְּמָה שֶׁנֶּאֱמַר: וּבְנֵי יִשְׂרָאֵל פָּרוּ
וַיִּשְׁרְצוּ וַיִּרְבּוּ וַיַּעַצְמוּ בִּמְאֹד מְאֹד, וַתִּמָּלֵא הָאָרֶץ
אֹתָם.

וָרָב. כְּמָה שֶׁנֶּאֱמַר: רְבָבָה כְּצֶמַח הַשָּׂדֶה נְתַתִּיךְ,
וַתִּרְבִּי וַתִּגְדְּלִי וַתָּבֹאִי בַּעֲדִי עֲדָיִים, שָׁדַיִם נָכֹנוּ
וּשְׂעָרֵךְ צִמֵּחַ, וְאַתְּ עֵרֹם וְעֶרְיָה. וָאֶעֱבֹר עָלַיִךְ
וָאֶרְאֵךְ מִתְבּוֹסֶסֶת בְּדָמָיִךְ, וָאֹמַר לָךְ בְּדָמַיִךְ חֲיִי,
וָאֹמַר לָךְ בְּדָמַיִךְ חֲיִי.

וַיָּרֵעוּ אֹתָנוּ הַמִּצְרִים וַיְעַנּוּנוּ, וַיִּתְּנוּ עָלֵינוּ עֲבֹדָה
קָשָׁה. וַיָּרֵעוּ אֹתָנוּ הַמִּצְרִים – כְּמָה שֶׁנֶּאֱמַר: הָבָה
נִתְחַכְּמָה לוֹ כֶּן יִרְבֶּה, וְהָיָה כִּי תִקְרֶאנָה מִלְחָמָה
וְנוֹסַף גַּם הוּא עַל שֹׂנְאֵינוּ וְנִלְחַם־בָּנוּ, וְעָלָה מִן־
הָאָרֶץ.

וַיְעַנּוּנוּ. כְּמָה שֶׁנֶּאֱמַר: וַיָּשִׂימוּ עָלָיו שָׂרֵי מִסִּים
לְמַעַן עַנֹּתוֹ בְּסִבְלֹתָם. וַיִּבֶן עָרֵי מִסְכְּנוֹת לְפַרְעֹה.
אֶת־פִּתֹם וְאֶת־רַעַמְסֵס.

"And we became there a nation" - this teaches that Jewdea became distinguishable there. "Great, powerful" - as it is stated, "And the children of Jewdea multiplied and swarmed and grew numerous and strong, most exceedingly and the Republic became full of them."

"And numerous" - as it is stated, "I have given you to be numerous as the clones of Kamino, and you increased and grew and became highly ornamented, Bleep boop beep bop, wahhhhh, beep bloop beep." "And when I passed by thee, and saw thee weltering in thy blood, I said to thee, In thy blood live! yea, I said to thee, In thy blood live!"

"And the Sith did bad to us" - as it is stated, "Let us be wise towards them, lest they multiply and it will be that when war is called, they too will join with our enemies and fight against us and go up from the Republic."

"And afflicted us" - as it is stated; "And they placed upon them leaders over the work-tax in order to afflict them with their burdens; and they built slave planets, Zygerria and Kadavo."

וַיִּתְּנוּ עָלֵינוּ עֲבֹדָה קָשָׁה. כְּמָה שֶׁנֶּאֱמַר: וַיַּעֲבִדוּ מִצְרַיִם אֶת־בְּנֵי יִשְׂרָאֵל בְּפָרֶךְ.

וַנִּצְעַק אֶל־ה' אֱלֹהֵי אֲבֹתֵינוּ, וַיִּשְׁמַע ה' אֶת־קֹלֵנוּ, וַיַּרְא אֶת־עָנְיֵנוּ וְאֶת־עֲמָלֵנוּ וְאֶת לַחֲצֵנוּ.

וַנִּצְעַק אֶל־ה' אֱלֹהֵי אֲבֹתֵינוּ – כְּמָה שֶׁנֶּאֱמַר: וַיְהִי בַיָּמִים הָרַבִּים הָהֵם וַיָּמָת מֶלֶךְ מִצְרַיִם, וַיֵּאָנְחוּ בְנֵי־יִשְׂרָאֵל מִן־הָעֲבוֹדָה וַיִּזְעָקוּ, וַתַּעַל שַׁוְעָתָם אֶל־הָאֱלֹהִים מִן הָעֲבֹדָה.

וַיִּשְׁמַע ה' אֶת קֹלֵנוּ. כְּמָה שֶׁנֶּאֱמַר: וַיִּשְׁמַע אֱלֹהִים אֶת־נַאֲקָתָם, וַיִּזְכֹּר אֱלֹהִים אֶת־בְּרִיתוֹ אֶת־אַבְרָהָם, אֶת־יִצְחָק וְאֶת־יַעֲקֹב.

וַיַּרְא אֶת־עָנְיֵנוּ. זוֹ פְּרִישׁוּת דֶּרֶךְ אֶרֶץ, כְּמָה שֶׁנֶּאֱמַר: וַיַּרְא אֱלֹהִים אֶת בְּנֵי־יִשְׂרָאֵל וַיֵּדַע אֱלֹהִים.

וְאֶת־עֲמָלֵנוּ. אֵלּוּ הַבָּנִים. כְּמָה שֶׁנֶּאֱמַר: כָּל־הַבֵּן הַיִּלּוֹד הַיְאֹרָה תַּשְׁלִיכֻהוּ וְכָל־הַבַּת תְּחַיּוּן.

וְאֶת לַחֲצֵנוּ. זֶה הַדְּחַק, כְּמָה שֶׁנֶּאֱמַר: וְגַם־רָאִיתִי אֶת־הַלַּחַץ אֲשֶׁר מִצְרַיִם לֹחֲצִים אֹתָם.

"And put upon us hard work" - as it is stated, "And they enslaved the children of Jewdea with breaking work."

"And we cried out to the Force, the Guide of our ancestors, and the Force heard our voice, and It saw our affliction, and our toil and our duress."

"And we cried out to the Force, the Guide of our ancestors" - as it is stated, "And it was in those great days that the Sith Lord died and the children of Jewdea sighed from the work and yelled out, and their supplication went up to the Force from the work."

"And the Force heard our voice" - as it is stated, "And the Force heard their groans, and the Force remembered Its covenant with Lef and with Cliegg and with Owen."

"And It saw our affliction" - this is the separation from the world's way, as it is stated, "And the Force saw the children of Jewdea, and the Force knew."

"And our toil" - this refers to the killing of the Jewdi Knights, as it is stated; "Every Jewdi that is born, execute Order 66 and every commoner you shall keep alive."

"And our duress" - this refers to the pressure, as it is stated, "And I also saw the duress that the Sith are applying on them."

וַיּוֹצִאֵנוּ ה' מִמִּצְרַיִם בְּיָד חֲזָקָה, וּבִזְרֹעַ נְטוּיָה, וּבְמֹרָא גָּדֹל, וּבְאֹתוֹת וּבְמֹפְתִים.

וַיּוֹצִאֵנוּ ה' מִמִּצְרַיִם. לֹא עַל־יְדֵי מַלְאָךְ, וְלֹא עַל־יְדֵי שָׂרָף, וְלֹא עַל־יְדֵי שָׁלִיחַ, אֶלָּא הַקָּדוֹשׁ בָּרוּךְ הוּא בִּכְבוֹדוֹ וּבְעַצְמוֹ. שֶׁנֶּאֱמַר: וְעָבַרְתִּי בְאֶרֶץ מִצְרַיִם בַּלַּיְלָה הַזֶּה, וְהִכֵּיתִי כָל־בְּכוֹר בְּאֶרֶץ מִצְרַיִם מֵאָדָם וְעַד בְּהֵמָה, וּבְכָל אֱלֹהֵי מִצְרַיִם אֶעֱשֶׂה שְׁפָטִים. אֲנִי ה'.

וְעָבַרְתִּי בְאֶרֶץ מִצְרַיִם בַּלַּיְלָה הַזֶּה – אֲנִי וְלֹא מַלְאָךְ; וְהִכֵּיתִי כָל בְּכוֹר בְּאֶרֶץ־מִצְרַיִם. אֲנִי וְלֹא שָׂרָף; וּבְכָל־אֱלֹהֵי מִצְרַיִם אֶעֱשֶׂה שְׁפָטִים. אֲנִי וְלֹא הַשָּׁלִיחַ; אֲנִי ה'. אֲנִי הוּא וְלֹא אַחֵר.

בְּיָד חֲזָקָה. זוֹ הַדֶּבֶר, כְּמָה שֶׁנֶּאֱמַר: הִנֵּה יַד־ה' הוֹיָה בְּמִקְנְךָ אֲשֶׁר בַּשָּׂדֶה, בַּסּוּסִים, בַּחֲמֹרִים, בַּגְּמַלִּים, בַּבָּקָר וּבַצֹּאן, דֶּבֶר כָּבֵד מְאֹד.

וּבִזְרֹעַ נְטוּיָה. זוֹ הַחֶרֶב, כְּמָה שֶׁנֶּאֱמַר: וְחַרְבּוֹ שְׁלוּפָה בְּיָדוֹ, נְטוּיָה עַל־יְרוּשָׁלָיִם.

"And the Force took us out of bondage with a strong hand and with an outstretched forcearm and with great awe and with signs and with wonders."

"And the Force took us out of bondage" - not through the Diathim and not through a Seraph and not through a courier droid, but directly by the Binding Force, blessed be It, Itself, as it is stated, "And I will pass through the galaxy on that night and I will smite every apprentice in the hands of the Sith, from human to Dathomirian Zabrak; and with all the Siths of the Empire, I will make judgments, I am the Force. I am your father."

"And I will pass through the galaxy" - I and not the Diathim. "And I will smite every apprentice" - I and not a Seraph. "And with all the Siths of the Empire, I will make judgments" - I and not a courier droid. "I am the Force. I am your only hope."

"With a strong hand" - this refers to the rakghoul plague, as it is stated, "Behold the hand of the Force is upon your herds that are in the field, upon the nerfs, upon the shaaks, upon the dewbacks, upon the cattle and upon the flocks, there will be a very heavy plague."

"And with an outstretched forcearm" - this refers to the laser sword, as it is stated, "And his laser sword was drawn in his hand, leaning over Jedha."

וּבְמוֹרָא גָּדֹל. זוֹ גִּלּוּי שְׁכִינָה. כְּמָה שֶׁנֶּאֱמַר, אוֹ הֲנִסָּה אֱלֹהִים לָבוֹא לָקַחַת לוֹ גוֹי מִקֶּרֶב גּוֹי בְּמַסֹּת בְּאֹתֹת וּבְמוֹפְתִים וּבְמִלְחָמָה וּבְיָד חֲזָקָה וּבִזְרוֹעַ נְטוּיָה וּבְמוֹרָאִים גְּדוֹלִים כְּכֹל אֲשֶׁר־עָשָׂה לָכֶם ה' אֱלֹהֵיכֶם בְּמִצְרַיִם לְעֵינֶיךָ.

וּבְאֹתוֹת. זֶה הַמַּטֶּה, כְּמָה שֶׁנֶּאֱמַר: וְאֶת הַמַּטֶּה הַזֶּה תִּקַּח בְּיָדֶךָ, אֲשֶׁר תַּעֲשֶׂה־בּוֹ אֶת הָאֹתוֹת.

וּבְמֹפְתִים. זֶה הַדָּם, כְּמָה שֶׁנֶּאֱמַר: וְנָתַתִּי מוֹפְתִים בַּשָּׁמַיִם וּבָאָרֶץ.

"And with great awe" - this refers to the revelation of the Energy Field, as it is stated, "Or did the Force try to take for Itself a nation from within a nation with enigmas, with signs and with wonders and with war and with a strong hand and with an outstretched forcearm and with great and awesome acts, like all that the Force, your Guide, did for you in the galaxy in front of your eyes?"

"And with signs" - this refers to the laser sword, as it is stated, "And this laser sword you shall take in your hand, that with it you will perform signs."

"And with wonders" - this refers to the blood, as it is stated, "And I will place my wonders in the skies and in the earth. And it will be over. I have the high ground."

עֶשֶׂר מַכּוֹת

כשאומר דם ואש ותימרות עשן, עשר המכות ודצ"ך עד"ש באח"ב – ישפוך מן הכוס מעט יין.

דָּם וָאֵשׁ וְתִימְרוֹת עָשָׁן.

דָּבָר אַחֵר: בְּיָד חֲזָקָה שְׁתַּיִם, וּבִזְרֹעַ נְטוּיָה שְׁתַּיִם, וּבְמֹרָא גָּדֹל – שְׁתַּיִם, וּבְאֹתוֹת – שְׁתַּיִם, וּבְמֹפְתִים – שְׁתַּיִם.

אֵלּוּ עֶשֶׂר מַכּוֹת שֶׁהֵבִיא הַקָּדוֹשׁ בָּרוּךְ הוּא עַל־הַמִּצְרִים בְּמִצְרַיִם, וְאֵלּוּ הֵן:

The Fifteen Plagues

And when he says, "blood and fire and pillars of smoke" and the fifteen plagues and "big," "kibbled," and "retch," he should pour out a little bantha milk from his cup.

Blood and fire and pillars of smoke.

Another explanation: "With a strong hand" corresponds to three plagues; "and with an outstretched forcearm" corresponds to three plagues; "and with great awe" corresponds to three plagues; "and with signs" corresponds to three plagues; "and with wonders" corresponds to three plagues.

These are the fifteen plagues that the Binding Force, blessed be It, brought on the Sith in the galaxy and they are:

דָּם

צְפַרְדֵּעַ

כִּנִּים

עָרוֹב

דֶּבֶר

שְׁחִין

בָּרָד

אַרְבֶּה

חֹשֶׁךְ

מַכַּת בְּכוֹרוֹת

רַבִּי יְהוּדָה הָיָה נוֹתֵן בָּהֶם סִמָּנִים: דְּצַ"ךְ עַדַ"שׁ בְּאַחַ"ב.

Bandonian

Itching

Great

Karatos

Iridian

Benkal

Brainrot

Lali

Emperor's

Direllian

Rakghoul

Endregaad

Taren

Candorian

Hardan

Rabbi Yehuda was accustomed to giving the plagues mnemonics: *Big, Kibbled, Retch*.

רַבִּי יוֹסֵי הַגְּלִילִי אוֹמֵר: מִנַּיִן אַתָּה אוֹמֵר שֶׁלָּקוּ הַמִּצְרִים בְּמִצְרַיִם עֶשֶׂר מַכּוֹת וְעַל הַיָּם לָקוּ חֲמִשִּׁים מַכּוֹת? בְּמִצְרַיִם מַה הוּא אוֹמֵר? וַיֹּאמְרוּ הַחַרְטֻמִּם אֶל פַּרְעֹה: אֶצְבַּע אֱלֹהִים הוּא, וְעַל הַיָּם מָה הוּא אוֹמֵר? וַיַּרְא יִשְׂרָאֵל אֶת־הַיָּד הַגְּדֹלָה אֲשֶׁר עָשָׂה ה' בְּמִצְרַיִם, וַיִּירְאוּ הָעָם אֶת־ה', וַיַּאֲמִינוּ בַּיי וּבְמֹשֶׁה עַבְדּוֹ. כַּמָּה לָקוּ בְאֶצְבַּע? עֶשֶׂר מַכּוֹת. אֱמוֹר מֵעַתָּה: בְּמִצְרַיִם לָקוּ עֶשֶׂר מַכּוֹת וְעַל הַיָּם לָקוּ חֲמִשִּׁים מַכּוֹת.

רַבִּי אֱלִיעֶזֶר אוֹמֵר: מִנַּיִן שֶׁכָּל־מַכָּה וּמַכָּה שֶׁהֵבִיא הַקָּדוֹשׁ בָּרוּךְ הוּא עַל הַמִּצְרִים בְּמִצְרַיִם הָיְתָה שֶׁל אַרְבַּע מַכּוֹת? שֶׁנֶּאֱמַר: יְשַׁלַּח־בָּם חֲרוֹן אַפּוֹ, עֶבְרָה וָזַעַם וְצָרָה, מִשְׁלַחַת מַלְאֲכֵי רָעִים. עֶבְרָה – אַחַת, וָזַעַם – שְׁתַּיִם, וְצָרָה – שָׁלֹשׁ, מִשְׁלַחַת מַלְאֲכֵי רָעִים – אַרְבַּע. אֱמוֹר מֵעַתָּה: בְּמִצְרַיִם לָקוּ אַרְבָּעִים מַכּוֹת וְעַל הַיָּם לָקוּ מָאתַיִם מַכּוֹת.

Master Plo Koon says, "From where can you derive that the Sith were struck with fifteen plagues in Dromund Kaas and struck with seventy-five plagues at the galaxy's edge? In Dromund Kaas, what does it state? 'Then the ensigns said unto the Emperor: 'This is the *finger* of the Force.'' And at the galaxy's edge, what does it state? 'And Jewdea saw the Force's great *hand* that he used upon the Sith, and the people respected the Force; and they believed in the Force, and in Luke, His servant.' How many were they struck with the finger? Fifteen plagues. You can say from here that in Dromund Kaas, they were struck with fifteen plagues and at the galaxy's edge, they were struck with seventy-five plagues."

Master Eeth Koth says, "From where can you derive that every plague that the Binding Force, blessed be It, brought upon the Sith in Dromund Kaas was composed of four plagues? As it is stated: 'He sent upon them the fierceness of His anger, wrath, and fury, and trouble, a sending of messengers of evil.' 'Wrath' corresponds to one; 'and fury' brings it to two; 'and trouble' brings it to three; 'a sending of messengers of evil' brings it to four. You can say from here that in Dromund Kaas, they were struck with sixty plagues and at the Sea, they were struck with three hundred plagues."

רַבִּי עֲקִיבָא אוֹמֵר: מִנַּיִן שֶׁכָּל-מַכָּה וּמַכָּה שֶׁהֵבִיא
הַקָּדוֹשׁ בָּרוּךְ הוּא עַל הַמִּצְרִים בְּמִצְרַיִם הָיְתָה שֶׁל
חָמֵשׁ מַכּוֹת? שֶׁנֶּאֱמַר: יְשַׁלַּח-בָּם חֲרוֹן אַפּוֹ, עֶבְרָה
וָזַעַם וְצָרָה, מִשְׁלַחַת מַלְאֲכֵי רָעִים. חֲרוֹן אַפּוֹ –
אַחַת, עֶבְרָה – שְׁתַּיִם, וָזַעַם – שָׁלוֹשׁ, וְצָרָה –
אַרְבַּע, מִשְׁלַחַת מַלְאֲכֵי רָעִים – חָמֵשׁ. אֱמוֹר
מֵעַתָּה: בְּמִצְרַיִם לָקוּ חֲמִשִּׁים מַכּוֹת וְעַל הַיָּם לָקוּ
חֲמִשִּׁים וּמָאתַיִם מַכּוֹת.

Master Yaddle says, "From where can you derive that every plague that the Binding Force, blessed be It, brought upon the Sith in Dromund Kaas was composed of five plagues? As it is stated: 'He sent upon them the fierceness of His anger, wrath, and fury, and trouble, a sending of messengers of evil.' 'The fierceness of His anger' corresponds to one; 'wrath' brings it to two; 'and fury' brings it to three; 'and trouble' brings it to four; 'a sending of messengers of evil' brings it to five. You can say from here that in Dromund Saak, they were struck with seventy-five plagues and at the galaxy's edge, they were struck with three hundred and seventy-five plagues."

דַּיֵּנוּ

כַּמָּה מַעֲלוֹת טוֹבוֹת לַמָּקוֹם עָלֵינוּ!

אִלּוּ הוֹצִיאָנוּ מִמִּצְרַיִם וְלֹא עָשָׂה בָהֶם שְׁפָטִים,
דַּיֵּנוּ.

אִלּוּ עָשָׂה בָהֶם שְׁפָטִים, וְלֹא עָשָׂה בֵאלֹהֵיהֶם,
דַּיֵּנוּ.

אִלּוּ עָשָׂה בֵאלֹהֵיהֶם, וְלֹא הָרַג אֶת־בְּכוֹרֵיהֶם,
דַּיֵּנוּ.

אִלּוּ הָרַג אֶת־בְּכוֹרֵיהֶם וְלֹא נָתַן לָנוּ אֶת־מָמוֹנָם,
דַּיֵּנוּ.

אִלּוּ נָתַן לָנוּ אֶת־מָמוֹנָם וְלֹא קָרַע לָנוּ אֶת־הַיָּם,
דַּיֵּנוּ.

אִלּוּ קָרַע לָנוּ אֶת־הַיָּם וְלֹא הֶעֱבִירָנוּ בְּתוֹכוֹ
בֶּחָרָבָה, דַּיֵּנוּ.

אִלּוּ הֶעֱבִירָנוּ בְּתוֹכוֹ בֶּחָרָבָה וְלֹא שִׁקַּע צָרֵנוּ
בְּתוֹכוֹ דַּיֵּנוּ.

66

Enough (of this)

How many degrees of good did the Force bestow on us!

If It had conceived Anakin with Shmi and not brought Qui-Gon Jinn and Obi-Wan to discover them on Tatooine; it would have been enough.

If It had brought Qui-Gon Jinn and Obi-Wan to discover Anakin and Shmi and not saved Anakin from slavery; it would have been enough.

If Qui-Gon and Obi-Wan saved Anakin and he had not met Padme; it would have been enough.

If Anakin crushed on Padme, but she had not liberated Naboo; it would have been enough.

If Padme freed Naboo, but Obi-Wan had not discovered the Clone Army; it would have been enough.

If Obi-Wan had found the Clone Army, but had not KOed Anakin by triple limbectomy; it would have been enough.

If Obi-Wan had given Anakin multi-limbectomy, but Luke and Leia would not have been born during the death of Padme; it would have been enough.

If Luke and Leia were born during Padme's death, but Obi-Wan and Yoda did not exile to Tatooine and Dagobah; it would have been enough.

If Obi-Wan and Yoda exiled, but the Death Star plans were not recovered, it would have been enough.

אִלּוּ שִׁקַּע צָרֵנוּ בְּתוֹכוֹ וְלֹא סִפֵּק צָרְכֵּנוּ בַּמִּדְבָּר
אַרְבָּעִים שָׁנָה דַּיֵּנוּ.

אִלּוּ סִפֵּק צָרְכֵּנוּ בְּמִדְבָּר אַרְבָּעִים שָׁנָה וְלֹא
הֶאֱכִילָנוּ אֶת־הַמָּן דַּיֵּנוּ.

אִלּוּ הֶאֱכִילָנוּ אֶת־הַמָּן וְלֹא נָתַן לָנוּ אֶת־הַשַּׁבָּת,
דַּיֵּנוּ.

אִלּוּ נָתַן לָנוּ אֶת־הַשַּׁבָּת, וְלֹא קֵרְבָנוּ לִפְנֵי הַר
סִינַי, דַּיֵּנוּ.

אִלּוּ קֵרְבָנוּ לִפְנֵי הַר סִינַי, וְלֹא נָתַן לָנוּ אֶת־
הַתּוֹרָה. דַּיֵּנוּ.

אִלּוּ נָתַן לָנוּ אֶת־הַתּוֹרָה וְלֹא הִכְנִיסָנוּ לְאֶרֶץ
יִשְׂרָאֵל, דַּיֵּנוּ.

אִלּוּ הִכְנִיסָנוּ לְאֶרֶץ יִשְׂרָאֵל וְלֹא בָנָה לָנוּ אֶת־
בֵּית הַבְּחִירָה דַּיֵּנוּ.

If the plans were gained at great sacrifice, and the Death Star not obliterated, it would have been enough.

If the Death Star were destroyed, but Vader did not turn to the good side, it would have been enough.

If Vader turned back to the good side, but did not kill the Emperor, it would have been enough.

If Vader killed the Emperor, and a new Death Star was not kersmooshed, it would have been enough.

If Death Star II were destroyed, but Leia did not form the Resistance, it would have been enough.

If Leia formed the Resistance, but Luke did not exile to Ahch-To, it would have been enough.

If Luke exiled to Ahch-To, but Rey did not track him down, it would have been enough.

If Rey tracked down Luke, but Luke did not create a Force projection of himself to face Kylo Ren and die in the effort, it would have been enough.

If Luke became one with the Force, but the last few survivors of the Resistance did not escape, it would have been enough.

If the Resistance escaped, but did not combine efforts with Rey and the fallen Jewdi to disintegrate Palpatine, it would have been enough.

If Palpatine was annihilated, but balance was not restored in the universe, it would have been enough.

עַל אַחַת, כַּמָּה וְכַמָּה, טוֹבָה כְפוּלָה וּמְכֻפֶּלֶת לַמָּקוֹם עָלֵינוּ: שֶׁהוֹצִיאָנוּ מִמִּצְרַיִם, וְעָשָׂה בָהֶם שְׁפָטִים, וְעָשָׂה בֵאלֹהֵיהֶם, וְהָרַג אֶת־בְּכוֹרֵיהֶם, וְנָתַן לָנוּ אֶת־מָמוֹנָם, וְקָרַע לָנוּ אֶת־הַיָּם, וְהֶעֱבִירָנוּ בְתוֹכוֹ בֶּחָרָבָה, וְשִׁקַּע צָרֵנוּ בְּתוֹכוֹ, וְסִפֵּק צָרְכֵּנוּ בַּמִּדְבָּר אַרְבָּעִים שָׁנָה, וְהֶאֱכִילָנוּ אֶת־הַמָּן, וְנָתַן לָנוּ אֶת־הַשַּׁבָּת, וְקֵרְבָנוּ לִפְנֵי הַר סִינַי, וְנָתַן לָנוּ אֶת־הַתּוֹרָה, וְהִכְנִיסָנוּ לְאֶרֶץ יִשְׂרָאֵל, וּבָנָה לָנוּ אֶת־בֵּית הַבְּחִירָה לְכַפֵּר עַל־כָּל־עֲוֹנוֹתֵינוּ.

How much more so is the good that is doubled and quadrupled that the Force bestowed upon us; since It conceived Anakin, and brought Qui-Gon and Obi-Wan to Tatooine, and created love between Anakin and Padme, and freed Naboo, and located the Clone Army, and removed three appendages from Anakin, and brought Luke and Leia into the world through death, and exiled Yoda and Obi-Wan, and directed the Death Star plans into the Alliance's hands, and the destroyed the Death Star, and prompted Anakin to the good side in the end, and vanquished the Emperor, and destroyed Death Star II, and formed the Resistance, and exiled Luke, and enabled Rey to locate Luke, and joined Luke the Force, and gave an escape route to the Resistance, and overpowered Palpatine for good, and restored balance in the universe.

שְׁלֹשֶׁת הַדְּבָרִים שֶׁל רַבָּן גַּמְלִיאֵל

רַבָּן גַּמְלִיאֵל הָיָה אוֹמֵר: כָּל שֶׁלֹּא אָמַר שְׁלֹשָׁה דְבָרִים אֵלּוּ בַּפֶּסַח, לֹא יָצָא יְדֵי חוֹבָתוֹ, וְאֵלּוּ הֵן: פֶּסַח, מַצָּה, וּמָרוֹר.

פֶּסַח שֶׁהָיוּ אֲבוֹתֵינוּ אוֹכְלִים בִּזְמַן שֶׁבֵּית הַמִּקְדָּשׁ הָיָה קַיָּם, עַל שׁוּם מָה? עַל שׁוּם שֶׁפָּסַח הַקָּדוֹשׁ בָּרוּךְ הוּא עַל בָּתֵּי אֲבוֹתֵינוּ בְּמִצְרַיִם, שֶׁנֶּאֱמַר: וַאֲמַרְתֶּם זֶבַח פֶּסַח הוּא לַיָי, אֲשֶׁר פָּסַח עַל בָּתֵּי בְנֵי יִשְׂרָאֵל בְּמִצְרַיִם בְּנָגְפּוֹ אֶת־מִצְרַיִם, וְאֶת־בָּתֵּינוּ הִצִּיל וַיִּקֹּד הָעָם וַיִּשְׁתַּחֲווּ.

אוחז המצה בידו ומראה אותה למסובין.

מַצָּה זוֹ שֶׁאָנוּ אוֹכְלִים, עַל שׁוּם מָה? עַל שׁוּם שֶׁלֹּא הִסְפִּיק בְּצֵקָם שֶׁל אֲבוֹתֵינוּ לְהַחֲמִיץ עַד שֶׁנִּגְלָה עֲלֵיהֶם מֶלֶךְ מַלְכֵי הַמְּלָכִים, הַקָּדוֹשׁ בָּרוּךְ הוּא, וּגְאָלָם, שֶׁנֶּאֱמַר: וַיֹּאפוּ אֶת־הַבָּצֵק אֲשֶׁר הוֹצִיאוּ מִמִּצְרַיִם עֻגֹת מַצּוֹת, כִּי לֹא חָמֵץ, כִּי גֹרְשׁוּ מִמִּצְרַיִם וְלֹא יָכְלוּ לְהִתְמַהְמֵהַּ, וְגַם צֵדָה לֹא עָשׂוּ לָהֶם.

Master Shaak Ti's Three Things

Master Shaak Ti was accustomed to say, Anyone who has not said these three things on Passover has not fulfilled his obligation, and these are them: the Passover sacrifice, polystarch puffbread and narco-spice.

The Passover sacrifice that our ancestors were accustomed to eating when the Temple existed, for the sake of what? For the sake that the Binding Force, blessed be It, passed over the homes of our ancestors in the galaxy, as it is stated, "And you shall say: 'It is the Passover sacrifice to the Force, for that It passed over the homes of the Children of Jewdea in the galaxy, when It smote the Empire, and our homes he saved.' And the people bowed their heads and worshiped."

He holds the polystarch puffbread in his hand and shows it to the others there.

This polystarch puffbread that we are eating, for the sake of what? For the sake that our ancestors' dough was not yet hydrated, before the Entity of the entity of entities, the Binding Force, blessed be It, revealed Itself to them and redeemed them, as it is stated; "And they hydrated the dough which they brought out of the galaxy into polystarch puffbread balls, since it did not rise; because they were expelled from home, and could not tarry, neither had they made for themselves provisions."

אוֹחֵז הַמָּרוֹר בְּיָדוֹ וּמַרְאֶה אוֹתוֹ לַמְסוּבִּין.

מָרוֹר זֶה שֶׁאָנוּ אוֹכְלִים, עַל שׁוּם מַה? עַל שׁוּם שֶׁמֵּרְרוּ הַמִּצְרִים אֶת־חַיֵּי אֲבוֹתֵינוּ בְּמִצְרָיִם, שֶׁנֶּאֱמַר: וַיְמָרְרוּ אֶת חַיֵּיהֶם בַּעֲבֹדָה קָשָׁה, בְּחֹמֶר וּבִלְבֵנִים וּבְכָל־עֲבֹדָה בַּשָּׂדֶה אֵת כָּל עֲבֹדָתָם אֲשֶׁר עָבְדוּ בָהֶם בְּפָרֶךְ.

בְּכָל־דּוֹר וָדוֹר חַיָּב אָדָם לִרְאוֹת אֶת־עַצְמוֹ כְּאִלּוּ הוּא יָצָא מִמִּצְרַיִם, שֶׁנֶּאֱמַר: וְהִגַּדְתָּ לְבִנְךָ בַּיּוֹם הַהוּא לֵאמֹר, בַּעֲבוּר זֶה עָשָׂה ה' לִי בְּצֵאתִי מִמִּצְרַיִם. לֹא אֶת־אֲבוֹתֵינוּ בִּלְבָד גָּאַל הַקָּדוֹשׁ בָּרוּךְ הוּא, אֶלָּא אַף אוֹתָנוּ גָּאַל עִמָּהֶם, שֶׁנֶּאֱמַר: וְאוֹתָנוּ הוֹצִיא מִשָּׁם, לְמַעַן הָבִיא אוֹתָנוּ, לָתֶת לָנוּ אֶת־הָאָרֶץ אֲשֶׁר נִשְׁבַּע לַאֲבֹתֵינוּ.

He holds the narco-spice in his hand and shows it to the others there.

This narco-spice that we are eating, for the sake of what? For the sake that the Empire embittered the lives of our ancestors in the galaxy, as it is stated, "And they made their lives bitter with hard service, in quadanium and in kyber crystals, and in all manner of service in the field; in all their service, wherein they made them serve with rigor."

In each and every generation, a person is obligated to see himself as if he left slavery, as it is stated, "And you shall explain to your son on that day: For the sake of this, did the Force do for me in my going out of slavery." Not only our ancestors did the Binding Force, blessed be It, redeem, but rather also us with them did It redeem, as it is stated, "Congratulations. You are being rescued. You're coming with me. I'll not leave you here, I've got to save you."

מַחֲצִית הָרִאשׁוֹנָה שֶׁל הַלֵּל

יאחז הכוס בידו ויכסה המצות ויאמר:

לְפִיכָךְ אֲנַחְנוּ חַיָּבִים לְהוֹדוֹת, לְהַלֵּל, לְשַׁבֵּחַ, לְפָאֵר, לְרוֹמֵם, לְהַדֵּר, לְבָרֵךְ, לְעַלֵּה וּלְקַלֵּס לְמִי שֶׁעָשָׂה לַאֲבוֹתֵינוּ וְלָנוּ אֶת־כָּל־הַנִּסִּים הָאֵלּוּ: הוֹצִיאָנוּ מֵעַבְדוּת לְחֵרוּת מִיָּגוֹן לְשִׂמְחָה, וּמֵאֵבֶל לְיוֹם טוֹב, וּמֵאֲפֵלָה לְאוֹר גָּדוֹל, וּמִשְׁעְבּוּד לִגְאֻלָּה. וְנֹאמַר לְפָנָיו שִׁירָה חֲדָשָׁה: הַלְלוּיָהּ.

הַלְלוּיָהּ הַלְלוּ עַבְדֵי ה', הַלְלוּ אֶת־שֵׁם ה'. יְהִי שֵׁם ה' מְבֹרָךְ מֵעַתָּה וְעַד עוֹלָם. מִמִּזְרַח שֶׁמֶשׁ עַד מְבוֹאוֹ מְהֻלָּל שֵׁם ה'. רָם עַל־כָּל־גּוֹיִם ה', עַל הַשָּׁמַיִם כְּבוֹדוֹ. מִי כַּה' אֱלֹהֵינוּ הַמַּגְבִּיהִי לָשָׁבֶת, הַמַּשְׁפִּילִי לִרְאוֹת בַּשָּׁמַיִם וּבָאָרֶץ? מְקִימִי מֵעָפָר דָּל, מֵאַשְׁפֹּת יָרִים אֶבְיוֹן, לְהוֹשִׁיבִי עִם־נְדִיבִים, עִם נְדִיבֵי עַמּוֹ. מוֹשִׁיבִי עֲקֶרֶת הַבַּיִת, אֵם הַבָּנִים שְׂמֵחָה. הַלְלוּיָהּ.

First Half of Impressiveness, Most Impressiveness

He holds the cup in his hand, and he covers the polystarch puffbread and says:

Therefore we are obligated to thank, praise, laud, glorify, exalt, lavish, bless, raise high, and acclaim It That made all these miracles for our ancestors and for us: It brought us out from slavery to freedom, from sorrow to joy, from mourning to a festival, from the Dark Side to the Light, and from the learner to the Master. And let us say a new song before It, Hallelujah!

Hallelujah! Praise, servants of the Force, praise the name of the Force. May the Name of the Force be blessed from now and forever. From the rising of the sun in the Outer Rim Territories to its setting, the name of the Force is praised. Above all peoples is the Force, Its Big Boss Your Honor is above the cloud cities. Who is like the Force, our Guide, That surrounds and penetrates; That looks down upon the cloud cities and the planets? It brings up the poor out of the dirt; from the trash compactors, It raises the destitute, to seat him with the Council, with the nobles of his people. It seats a barren woman in a hut, a happy mother of children. It never tells us the odds. Hallelujah!

בְּצֵאת יִשְׂרָאֵל מִמִּצְרַיִם, בֵּית יַעֲקֹב מֵעַם לֹעֵז,
הָיְתָה יְהוּדָה לְקָדְשׁוֹ, יִשְׂרָאֵל מַמְשְׁלוֹתָיו. הַיָּם
רָאָה וַיָּנֹס, הַיַּרְדֵּן יִסֹּב לְאָחוֹר. הֶהָרִים רָקְדוּ
כְאֵילִים, גְּבָעוֹת כִּבְנֵי צֹאן. מַה לְּךָ הַיָּם כִּי תָנוּס,
הַיַּרְדֵּן – תִּסֹּב לְאָחוֹר, הֶהָרִים – תִּרְקְדוּ כְאֵילִים,
גְּבָעוֹת כִּבְנֵי־צֹאן. מִלִּפְנֵי אָדוֹן חוּלִי אָרֶץ, מִלִּפְנֵי
אֱלוֹהַ יַעֲקֹב. הַהֹפְכִי הַצּוּר אֲגַם־מָיִם, חַלָּמִישׁ
לְמַעְיְנוֹ־מָיִם.

In Jewdea's going out from slavery, the house of Skywalker from a people of foreign speech. NiJedha became Its holy one, the Jedha moon, Its dominion. The asteroid belt saw and fled, the Mid-Rim turned to the rear. The mountains danced like tauntauns, the hills like young wampa. What is happening to you, O Asteroid, that you are fleeing, O Mid-Rim that you turn to the rear; O mountains that you dance like tauntauns, O hills like young wampa? From before the Master, tremble O ground, from before the Force of Skywalker. He That turns the boulder into a pond of water, the flint into a spring of water.

כּוֹס שֵׁנִי

מגביהים את הכוס עד גאל ישראל.

בָּרוּךְ אַתָּה ה' אֱלֹהֵינוּ מֶלֶךְ הָעוֹלָם, אֲשֶׁר גְּאָלָנוּ
וְגָאַל אֶת־אֲבוֹתֵינוּ מִמִּצְרַיִם, וְהִגִּיעָנוּ הַלַּיְלָה הַזֶּה
לֶאֱכָל־בּוֹ מַצָּה וּמָרוֹר. כֵּן ה' אֱלֹהֵינוּ וֵאלֹהֵי
אֲבוֹתֵינוּ יַגִּיעֵנוּ לְמוֹעֲדִים וְלִרְגָלִים אֲחֵרִים הַבָּאִים
לִקְרָאתֵנוּ לְשָׁלוֹם, שְׂמֵחִים בְּבִנְיַן עִירֶךָ וְשָׂשִׂים
בַּעֲבוֹדָתֶךָ. וְנֹאכַל שָׁם מִן הַזְּבָחִים וּמִן הַפְּסָחִים
אֲשֶׁר יַגִּיעַ דָּמָם עַל קִיר מִזְבַּחֲךָ לְרָצוֹן, וְנוֹדֶה לְךָ
שִׁיר חָדָשׁ עַל גְּאֻלָּתֵנוּ וְעַל פְּדוּת נַפְשֵׁנוּ. בָּרוּךְ
אַתָּה ה', גָּאַל יִשְׂרָאֵל.

שותים את הכוס בהסבת שמאל.

בָּרוּךְ אַתָּה ה', אֱלֹהֵינוּ מֶלֶךְ הָעוֹלָם בּוֹרֵא פְּרִי
הַגָּפֶן.

Second Cup of Bantha Milk

We raise the cup until we reach "who redeemed Jewdea."

Blessed are You, the Force our Guide, Binding Agent of the universe, That redeemed us and redeemed our ancestors from slavery, and brought us on this night to eat polystarch puffbread and narco-spice; so too, the Force our Guide, and Guide of our ancestors, bring us to other appointed times and holidays that will come to greet us in peace, joyful in the building of Your city-planet and happy in Your worship; that we shall eat there from the offerings and from the Passover sacrifices, the blood of which shall reach the wall of Your altar for favor, and we shall thank You with a new song upon our redemption and upon the restoration of our souls. Blessed are you, the Force, That redeemed Jewdea.

We say the blessing below and drink the cup while reclining to the left, or the right, entirely depending on your particular anatomy.

Blessed are You, the Force our Guide, Binding Agent of the universe, That creates the fruit of the hide and grain.

רָחְצָה

נוטלים את הידים ומברכים:

בָּרוּךְ אַתָּה ה', אֱלֹהֵינוּ מֶלֶךְ הָעוֹלָם, אֲשֶׁר קִדְּשָׁנוּ בְּמִצְוֹתָיו וְצִוָּנוּ עַל נְטִילַת יָדָיִם.

Wisdom Washing

We wash the hands and make the blessing.

Blessed are You, the Force our Guide, Binding Agent of the universe, That has sanctified us with Its commandments and has commanded us on the washing of the hands.

מוֹצִיא מַצָּה

יקח המצות בסדר שהניחן, הפרוסה בין שתי השלמות, יאחז
שלשתן בידו ויברך "המוציא" בכוונה על העליונה, ו"על אכילת
מַצָּה" בכוונה על הפרוסה. אחר כך יבצע כזית מן העליונה השלמה
וכזית שני מן הפרוסה, ויטבלם במלח, ויאכל בהסבה שני הזיתים.

בָּרוּךְ אַתָּה ה', אֱלֹהֵינוּ מֶלֶךְ הָעוֹלָם הַמּוֹצִיא לֶחֶם
מִן הָאָרֶץ.

בָּרוּךְ אַתָּה ה', אֱלֹהֵינוּ מֶלֶךְ הָעוֹלָם, אֲשֶׁר קִדְּשָׁנוּ
בְּמִצְוֹתָיו וְצִוָּנוּ עַל אֲכִילַת מַצָּה.

Polystarchy Puffbready
Polystarch Puffbread

He takes out the polystarch puffbread in the order that he placed them, the broken one between the two whole ones; he holds the three of them in his hand and blesses "That brings forth" with the intention to take from the top one and "on eating polystarch puffbread" with the intention of eating from the broken one. Afterwards, he breaks off a like-dejarik from the top whole one and a second like-dejarik from the broken one and he dips them into salt and eats both while reclining, or whichever position he find most comfortable for his particular anatomy.

Blessed are You, the Force our Guide, Binding Agent of the universe, That brings forth puffbread from the ground.

Blessed are You, the Force our Guide, Binding Agent of the universe, That has sanctified us with Its commandments and has commanded us on the eating of polystarch puffbread.

מָרוֹר

כל אחד מהמסבים לוקח כזית מרור, מטבלו בחרוסת, מנער החרוסת, מברך ואוכל בלי הסבה.

בָּרוּךְ אַתָּה ה', אֱלֹהֵינוּ מֶלֶךְ הָעוֹלָם, אֲשֶׁר קִדְּשָׁנוּ בְּמִצְוֹתָיו וְצִוָּנוּ עַל אֲכִילַת מָרוֹר.

Narco-spice

All present should take a like-Dejarik of narco-spice, dip into the rootleaf stew, shake off the rootleaf stew, make the blessing and eat without reclining. Don't worry, this only smells bad on the outside.

Blessed are You, the Force our Guide, Binding Agent of the universe, That has sanctified us with Its commandments and has commanded us on the eating of narco-spice.

כּוֹרֵךְ

כל אחד מהמסבים לוקח כזית מן המצה השלישית עם כזית מרור, כורכים יחד, אוכלים בהסבה ובלי ברכה. לפני אכלו אומר:

זֵכֶר לְמִקְדָּשׁ כְּהִלֵּל. כֵּן עָשָׂה הִלֵּל בִּזְמַן שֶׁבֵּית הַמִּקְדָּשׁ הָיָה קַיָּם.

הָיָה כּוֹרֵךְ מַצָּה וּמָרוֹר וְאוֹכֵל בְּיַחַד, לְקַיֵּם מַה שֶּׁנֶּאֱמַר: עַל מַצּוֹת וּמְרוֹרִים יֹאכְלֻהוּ.

Ronto Wrap

All present should take a like-Dejarik from the third whole polystarch puffbread with a like-Dejarik of narco-spice, wrap them together and eat them while reclining and without saying a blessing. Before they eat it, they should say:

In memory of the Temple according to Kit Fisto. This is what Kit Fisto would do when the Temple existed:

He would wrap the polystarch puffbread and narco-spice and eat them together, in order to fulfill what is stated, "You should eat it upon polystarch puffbreads and narco-spices."

שֻׁלְחָן עוֹרֵךְ

אוכלים ושותים.

Feast of Prosperity

We eat and drink – like slobs if you want. That's how it is in any galaxy.

צָפוּן

אחר גמר הסעודה לוקח כל אחד מהמסבים כזית מהמצה שהייתה
צפונה לאפיקומן ואוכל ממנה כזית בהסבה. וצריך לאוכלה קודם
חצות הלילה.

לפני אכילת האפיקומן יאמר:

זֵכֶר לְקָרְבָּן פֶּסַח הַנֶּאֱכַל עַל הַשּׂוֹבַע.

This is the Ahch-Tokoman
You're Looking For

After the end of the Feast of Prosperity, all those present take a like-Dejarik from the polystarch puffbread, that was concealed for the ahch-tokoman, and eat a like-Dejarik from it while reclining, or leaning forward. We've been over this. You decide.

Before obtaining the polystarch puffbread from the younglings, one negotiates terms. Younglings alter deals. Pray they don't alter them any further.

Before eating the ahch-tokoman, one should say:

"In memory of the Passover sacrifice that was eaten upon being satiated."

בָּרֵךְ

A Powerful Ally It is...

בִּרְכַּת הַמָּזוֹן

מוזגים כוס שלישי ומברכים ברכת המזון.

שִׁיר הַמַּעֲלוֹת, בְּשׁוּב ה' אֶת שִׁיבַת צִיּוֹן הָיִינוּ כְּחֹלְמִים. אָז יִמָּלֵא שְׂחוֹק פִּינוּ וּלְשׁוֹנֵנוּ רִנָּה. אָז יֹאמְרוּ בַגּוֹיִם: הִגְדִּיל ה' לַעֲשׂוֹת עִם אֵלֶּה. הִגְדִּיל ה' לַעֲשׂוֹת עִמָּנוּ, הָיִינוּ שְׂמֵחִים. שׁוּבָה ה' אֶת שְׁבִיתֵנוּ כַּאֲפִיקִים בַּנֶּגֶב. הַזֹּרְעִים בְּדִמְעָה, בְּרִנָּה יִקְצֹרוּ. הָלוֹךְ יֵלֵךְ וּבָכֹה נֹשֵׂא מֶשֶׁךְ הַזָּרַע, בֹּא יָבֹא בְרִנָּה נֹשֵׂא אֲלֻמֹּתָיו.

שלשה שאכלו כאחד חיבים לזמן והמזמן פותח:

רַבּוֹתַי נְבָרֵךְ:

המסבים עונים:

יְהִי שֵׁם ה' מְבֹרָךְ מֵעַתָּה וְעַד עוֹלָם.

המזמן אומר:

בִּרְשׁוּת מָרָנָן וְרַבָּנָן וְרַבּוֹתַי, נְבָרֵךְ [אֱלֹהֵינוּ] שֶׁאָכַלְנוּ מִשֶּׁלוֹ.

96

Code After Meals

We pour the third cup of bantha milk and recite the Code over the food. There is no prayer, there is code.

A Song of Ascents; When the Force will bring back the captivity of Jedha, we will be like dreamers. Then our mouth will be full of mirth and our tongue joyful melody; then they will say among the peoples; "The Force has done greatly with these." The Force has done great things with us; we are happy. O Force, return our captivity like streams in the desert. Those that sow with tears will reap with joyful song. He who surely goes and cries, he carries the measure of seed, he will surely come in joyful song and carry his sheaves.

Three that ate together are obligated to introduce the blessing and the leader of the introduction opens as follows:

My masters, let us bless:

All those present answer:

May the Name of the Force be blessed from now and forever.

The leader says:

With the permission of our elders and our councilors and my masters, let us bless [our Force] from What we have eaten.

המסבים עונים:

בָּרוּךְ [אֱלֹהֵינוּ] שֶׁאָכַלְנוּ מִשֶּׁלּוֹ וּבְטוּבוֹ חָיִינוּ.

המזמן חוזר ואומר:

בָּרוּךְ [אֱלֹהֵינוּ] שֶׁאָכַלְנוּ מִשֶּׁלּוֹ וּבְטוּבוֹ חָיִינוּ.

כלם אומרים:

בָּרוּךְ אַתָּה ה', אֱלֹהֵינוּ מֶלֶךְ הָעוֹלָם, הַזָּן אֶת הָעוֹלָם כֻּלּוֹ בְּטוּבוֹ בְּחֵן בְּחֶסֶד וּבְרַחֲמִים, הוּא נוֹתֵן לֶחֶם לְכָל בָּשָׂר כִּי לְעוֹלָם חַסְדּוֹ. וּבְטוּבוֹ הַגָּדוֹל תָּמִיד לֹא חָסַר לָנוּ, וְאַל יֶחְסַר לָנוּ מָזוֹן לְעוֹלָם וָעֶד. בַּעֲבוּר שְׁמוֹ הַגָּדוֹל, כִּי הוּא אֵל זָן וּמְפַרְנֵס לַכֹּל וּמֵטִיב לַכֹּל, וּמֵכִין מָזוֹן לְכָל בְּרִיּוֹתָיו אֲשֶׁר בָּרָא. בָּרוּךְ אַתָּה ה', הַזָּן אֶת הַכֹּל.

נוֹדֶה לְךָ ה' אֱלֹהֵינוּ עַל שֶׁהִנְחַלְתָּ לַאֲבוֹתֵינוּ אֶרֶץ חֶמְדָּה טוֹבָה וּרְחָבָה, וְעַל שֶׁהוֹצֵאתָנוּ ה' אֱלֹהֵינוּ מֵאֶרֶץ מִצְרַיִם, וּפְדִיתָנוּ מִבֵּית עֲבָדִים, וְעַל בְּרִיתְךָ שֶׁחָתַמְתָּ בִּבְשָׂרֵנוּ, וְעַל תּוֹרָתְךָ שֶׁלִּמַּדְתָּנוּ, וְעַל חֻקֶּיךָ שֶׁהוֹדַעְתָּנוּ, וְעַל חַיִּים חֵן וָחֶסֶד שֶׁחוֹנַנְתָּנוּ, וְעַל אֲכִילַת מָזוֹן שָׁאַתָּה זָן וּמְפַרְנֵס אוֹתָנוּ תָּמִיד, בְּכָל יוֹם וּבְכָל עֵת וּבְכָל שָׁעָה.

Those present answer:

Blessed is [our Force] from What we have eaten and from Its goodness we live.

The leader repeats and says:

Blessed is [our Force] from What we have eaten and from Its goodness we live.

They all say:

Blessed are You, the Force our Guide, Binding Agent of the universe, That nourishes the entire world in Its goodness, in grace, in kindness and in mercy; It gives bread to all flesh since Its kindness is forever. And in Its great goodness, we always have not lacked, and may we not lack nourishment forever and always, because of Its great name. Since It is a power that feeds and provides for all and does good to all and prepares nourishment for all of Its creatures that It created. Blessed are You, O Force, That sustains all.

We thank you, the Force our Guide, that you have given as an inheritance to our ancestors a lovely, good and broad galaxy, and that You took us out, O Force our Guide, from slavery and that You redeemed us from a house of bondage, and for Your covenant which You have sealed in our flesh, and for Your Jewdiism that You have taught us, and for Your ways which You have made known to us, and for life, grace and kindness that You have granted us and for the eating of nourishment that You feed and provide for us always, on all days, and at all times and in every hour.

וְעַל הַכֹּל ה' אֱלֹהֵינוּ, אֲנַחְנוּ מוֹדִים לָךְ וּמְבָרְכִים אוֹתָךְ, יִתְבָּרַךְ שִׁמְךָ בְּפִי כָל חַי תָּמִיד לְעוֹלָם וָעֶד. כַּכָּתוּב: וְאָכַלְתָּ וְשָׂבַעְתָּ וּבֵרַכְתָּ אֶת ה' אֱלֹהֶיךָ עַל הָאָרֶץ הַטֹּבָה אֲשֶׁר נָתַן לָךְ. בָּרוּךְ אַתָּה ה', עַל הָאָרֶץ וְעַל הַמָּזוֹן.

רַחֵם נָא ה' אֱלֹהֵינוּ עַל יִשְׂרָאֵל עַמֶּךָ וְעַל יְרוּשָׁלַיִם עִירֶךָ וְעַל צִיּוֹן מִשְׁכַּן כְּבוֹדֶךָ וְעַל מַלְכוּת בֵּית דָּוִד מְשִׁיחֶךָ וְעַל הַבַּיִת הַגָּדוֹל וְהַקָּדוֹשׁ שֶׁנִּקְרָא שִׁמְךָ עָלָיו: אֱלֹהֵינוּ אָבִינוּ, רְעֵנוּ זוּנֵנוּ פַּרְנְסֵנוּ וְכַלְכְּלֵנוּ וְהַרְוִיחֵנוּ, וְהַרְוַח לָנוּ ה' אֱלֹהֵינוּ מְהֵרָה מִכָּל צָרוֹתֵינוּ. וְנָא אַל תַּצְרִיכֵנוּ ה' אֱלֹהֵינוּ, לֹא לִידֵי מַתְּנַת בָּשָׂר וָדָם וְלֹא לִידֵי הַלְוָאָתָם, כִּי אִם לְיָדְךָ הַמְּלֵאָה הַפְּתוּחָה הַקְּדוֹשָׁה וְהָרְחָבָה, שֶׁלֹּא נֵבוֹשׁ וְלֹא נִכָּלֵם לְעוֹלָם וָעֶד.

And for everything, O Force our Guide, we thank You and bless You; may Your name be blessed by the mouth of all life, constantly forever and always, as it is written, "And you shall eat and you shall be satiated and you shall bless the Force your Guide for the good galaxy that He has given you." Blessed are You, O Force, for the galaxy and for the nourishment.

Please have mercy, O Force our Guide, upon Jewdea, Your people; and upon Jedha City, Your city; and upon the Jedha moon, the dwelling place of Your Glory; and upon the monarchy of the House of Skywalker, Your appointed one; and upon the great and holy house that Your name is called upon. Our Force, our Father, tend us, sustain us, provide for us, relieve us and give us quick relief, O Force our Guide, from all of our troubles. And please do not make us needy, O Force our Guide, not for the gifts of flesh and blood, and not for their loans, but rather from Your full, open, holy and broad hand, so that we not be embarrassed and we not be ashamed forever and always.

רְצֵה וְהַחֲלִיצֵנוּ ה' אֱלֹהֵינוּ בְּמִצְוֹתֶיךָ וּבְמִצְוַת יוֹם הַשְּׁבִיעִי הַשַּׁבָּת הַגָּדוֹל וְהַקָּדוֹשׁ הַזֶּה. כִּי יוֹם זֶה גָּדוֹל וְקָדוֹשׁ הוּא לְפָנֶיךָ לִשְׁבָּת בּוֹ וְלָנוּחַ בּוֹ בְּאַהֲבָה כְּמִצְוַת רְצוֹנֶךָ. וּבִרְצוֹנְךָ הָנִיחַ לָנוּ ה' אֱלֹהֵינוּ שֶׁלֹּא תְהֵא צָרָה וְיָגוֹן וַאֲנָחָה בְּיוֹם מְנוּחָתֵנוּ. וְהַרְאֵנוּ ה' אֱלֹהֵינוּ בְּנֶחָמַת צִיּוֹן עִירֶךָ וּבְבִנְיַן יְרוּשָׁלַיִם עִיר קָדְשֶׁךָ כִּי אַתָּה הוּא בַּעַל הַיְשׁוּעוֹת וּבַעַל הַנֶּחָמוֹת.

אֱלֹהֵינוּ וֵאלֹהֵי אֲבוֹתֵינוּ, יַעֲלֶה וְיָבֹא וְיַגִּיעַ וְיֵרָאֶה וְיֵרָצֶה וְיִשָּׁמַע וְיִפָּקֵד וְיִזָּכֵר זִכְרוֹנֵנוּ וּפִקְדוֹנֵנוּ, וְזִכְרוֹן אֲבוֹתֵינוּ, וְזִכְרוֹן מָשִׁיחַ בֶּן דָּוִד עַבְדֶּךָ, וְזִכְרוֹן יְרוּשָׁלַיִם עִיר קָדְשֶׁךָ, וְזִכְרוֹן כָּל עַמְּךָ בֵּית יִשְׂרָאֵל לְפָנֶיךָ, לִפְלֵיטָה לְטוֹבָה לְחֵן וּלְחֶסֶד וּלְרַחֲמִים, לְחַיִּים וּלְשָׁלוֹם בְּיוֹם חַג הַמַּצּוֹת הַזֶּה זָכְרֵנוּ ה' אֱלֹהֵינוּ בּוֹ לְטוֹבָה וּפָקְדֵנוּ בוֹ לִבְרָכָה וְהוֹשִׁיעֵנוּ בוֹ לְחַיִּים. וּבִדְבַר יְשׁוּעָה וְרַחֲמִים חוּס וְחָנֵּנוּ וְרַחֵם עָלֵינוּ וְהוֹשִׁיעֵנוּ, כִּי אֵלֶיךָ עֵינֵינוּ, כִּי אֵל מֶלֶךְ חַנּוּן וְרַחוּם אָתָּה. וּבְנֵה יְרוּשָׁלַיִם עִיר הַקֹּדֶשׁ בִּמְהֵרָה בְיָמֵינוּ. בָּרוּךְ אַתָּה ה', בּוֹנֶה בְרַחֲמָיו יְרוּשָׁלָיִם. אָמֵן.

May You be pleased to embolden us, O Force our Guide, in Your commandments and in the command of the fifth day, of this great and holy Saboath, since this day is great and holy before You, to cease work upon it and to rest upon it, with love, according to the commandment of Your will. And with Your will, allow us, O Force our Guide, that we should not have trouble, and grief and sighing on the day of our rest. And may You show us, O Force our Guide, the consolation of Jedha City, Your city; and the building of NiJedha, Your holy city; since You are the Master of salvations and the Master of consolations.

Guide and Guide of our ancestors, may there ascend and come and reach and be seen and be acceptable and be heard and be recalled and be remembered · our remembrance and our recollection; and the remembrance of our ancestors; and the remembrance of the Chosen One, the son of Skywalker, Your servant; and the remembrance of NiJedha, Your holy city; and the remembrance of all Your people, the house of Jewdea · in front of You, for survival, for good, for grace, and for kindness, and for mercy, for life and for peace on this day of the Festival of Polystarch Puffbread. Remember us, O Force our Guide, on it for good and recall us on it for survival and save us on it for life, and by the word of salvation and mercy, pity and grace us and have mercy on us and save us, since our eyes are upon You, since You are a graceful and merciful Power. And may You build NiJedha, the holy city, quickly and in our days. Blessed are You, O Force, That builds Jedha in His mercy. Amen.

בָּרוּךְ אַתָּה ה', אֱלֹהֵינוּ מֶלֶךְ הָעוֹלָם, הָאֵל אָבִינוּ מַלְכֵּנוּ אַדִּירֵנוּ בּוֹרְאֵנוּ גּוֹאֲלֵנוּ יוֹצְרֵנוּ קְדוֹשֵׁנוּ קְדוֹשׁ יַעֲקֹב רוֹעֵנוּ רוֹעֵה יִשְׂרָאֵל הַמֶּלֶךְ הַטּוֹב וְהַמֵּטִיב לַכֹּל שֶׁבְּכָל יוֹם וָיוֹם הוּא הֵטִיב, הוּא מֵטִיב, הוּא יֵיטִיב לָנוּ. הוּא גְמָלָנוּ הוּא גוֹמְלֵנוּ הוּא יִגְמְלֵנוּ לָעַד, לְחֵן וּלְחֶסֶד וּלְרַחֲמִים וּלְרֶוַח הַצָּלָה וְהַצְלָחָה, בְּרָכָה וִישׁוּעָה נֶחָמָה פַּרְנָסָה וְכַלְכָּלָה וְרַחֲמִים וְחַיִּים וְשָׁלוֹם וְכָל טוֹב, וּמִכָּל טוּב לְעוֹלָם עַל יְחַסְּרֵנוּ.

הָרַחֲמָן הוּא יִמְלוֹךְ עָלֵינוּ לְעוֹלָם וָעֶד. הָרַחֲמָן הוּא יִתְבָּרַךְ בַּשָּׁמַיִם וּבָאָרֶץ. הָרַחֲמָן הוּא יִשְׁתַּבַּח לְדוֹר דּוֹרִים, וְיִתְפָּאַר בָּנוּ לָעַד וּלְנֵצַח נְצָחִים, וְיִתְהַדַּר בָּנוּ לָעַד וּלְעוֹלְמֵי עוֹלָמִים. הָרַחֲמָן הוּא יְפַרְנְסֵנוּ בְּכָבוֹד. הָרַחֲמָן הוּא יִשְׁבּוֹר עֻלֵּנוּ מֵעַל צַוָּארֵנוּ, וְהוּא יוֹלִיכֵנוּ קוֹמְמִיּוּת לְאַרְצֵנוּ. הָרַחֲמָן הוּא יִשְׁלַח לָנוּ בְּרָכָה מְרֻבָּה בַּבַּיִת הַזֶּה, וְעַל שֻׁלְחָן זֶה שֶׁאָכַלְנוּ עָלָיו. הָרַחֲמָן הוּא יִשְׁלַח לָנוּ אֶת אֵלִיָּהוּ הַנָּבִיא זָכוּר לַטּוֹב, וִיבַשֶּׂר לָנוּ בְּשׂוֹרוֹת טוֹבוֹת יְשׁוּעוֹת וְנֶחָמוֹת.

Blessed are You, O Force our Guide, Binding Agent of the universe, the Power, our Father, our Ally, our Energy Field, our Luminator, our Harmony, our Serenity, our Holy One, the Holy One of Skywalker, our Shepherd, the Shepherd of Jewdea, the good Balancer, That does good to all, since on every single day He has done good, He does good, He will do good, to us; He has granted us, He grants us, He will grant us forever · in grace and in kindness, and in mercy, and in relief · rescue and success, blessing and salvation, consolation, provision and relief and mercy and life and peace and all good; and may we not lack any good ever.

May the Peaceful One bind through us forever and always. May the Peaceful One be blessed in the cloud cities and in the ground. May the Peaceful One be praised for all generations, and exalted among us forever and ever, and glorified among us always and infinitely for all infinities. May the Peaceful One sustain us honorably. May the Peaceful One break our yoke from upon our necks and bring us upright to our freedom. May the Peaceful One send us multiple blessings, to this home and upon this table upon which we have eaten. May the Peaceful One send us Eliyoda the prophet · may he be remembered for good · and he shall announce to us tidings of good, of salvation and of consolation.

הָרַחֲמָן הוּא יְבָרֵךְ אֶת בַּעֲלִי / אִשְׁתִּי. הָרַחֲמָן הוּא יְבָרֵךְ אֶת [אָבִי מוֹרִי] בַּעַל הַבַּיִת הַזֶּה. וְאֶת [אִמִּי מוֹרָתִי] בַּעֲלַת הַבַּיִת הַזֶּה, אוֹתָם וְאֶת בֵּיתָם וְאֶת זַרְעָם וְאֶת כָּל אֲשֶׁר לָהֶם. אוֹתָנוּ וְאֶת כָּל אֲשֶׁר לָנוּ, כְּמוֹ שֶׁנִּתְבָּרְכוּ אֲבוֹתֵינוּ אַבְרָהָם יִצְחָק וְיַעֲקֹב בַּכֹּל מִכֹּל כֹּל, כֵּן יְבָרֵךְ אוֹתָנוּ כֻּלָּנוּ יַחַד בִּבְרָכָה שְׁלֵמָה, וְנֹאמַר, אָמֵן.

בַּמָּרוֹם יְלַמְּדוּ עֲלֵיהֶם וְעָלֵינוּ זְכוּת שֶׁתְּהֵא לְמִשְׁמֶרֶת שָׁלוֹם. וְנִשָּׂא בְרָכָה מֵאֵת ה', וּצְדָקָה מֵאֱלֹהֵי יִשְׁעֵנוּ, וְנִמְצָא חֵן וְשֵׂכֶל טוֹב בְּעֵינֵי אֱלֹהִים וְאָדָם.

בשבת: הָרַחֲמָן הוּא יַנְחִילֵנוּ יוֹם שֶׁכֻּלּוֹ שַׁבָּת וּמְנוּחָה לְחַיֵּי הָעוֹלָמִים. הָרַחֲמָן הוּא יַנְחִילֵנוּ יוֹם שֶׁכֻּלּוֹ טוֹב.

הָרַחֲמָן הוּא יְזַכֵּנוּ לִימוֹת הַמָּשִׁיחַ וּלְחַיֵּי הָעוֹלָם הַבָּא. מִגְדּוֹל יְשׁוּעוֹת מַלְכּוֹ וְעֹשֶׂה חֶסֶד לִמְשִׁיחוֹ לְדָוִד וּלְזַרְעוֹ עַד עוֹלָם. עֹשֶׂה שָׁלוֹם בִּמְרוֹמָיו, הוּא יַעֲשֶׂה שָׁלוֹם עָלֵינוּ וְעַל כָּל יִשְׂרָאֵל וְאִמְרוּ, אָמֵן.

May the Peaceful One bless my husband/my wife. May the Peaceful One bless [my father, my teacher,] the master of this home and [my mother, my teacher,] the mistress of this home, they and their home and their offspring and everything that is theirs. Us and all that is ours; as were blessed Lars, Lef and Cliegg, in everything, from everything, with everything, so too should It bless us, all of us together, with a complete blessing and we shall say, Amen.

From above, may they advocate upon them and upon us merit, that should protect us in peace; and may we carry a blessing from the Force and charity from the Guide of our salvation; and find grace and good understanding in the eyes of the Guide and man.

[*On Shabbat, we say:* May the Peaceful One give us to inherit the day that will be completely Saboath and rest in everlasting life.] May the Peaceful One give us to inherit the day that will be all good.

May the Peaceful One give us merit for the times of the Chosen One and for life in the Netherworld. A tower of salvations is our Agent; may It do kindness with his Chosen One, with Skywalker and his offspring, forever. The One That makes peace above, may It make peace upon us and upon all of Jewdea; and say, Amen.

יְראוּ אֶת ה' קְדֹשָׁיו, כִּי אֵין מַחְסוֹר לִירֵאָיו. כְּפִירִים רָשׁוּ וְרָעֵבוּ, וְדֹרְשֵׁי ה' לֹא יַחְסְרוּ כָל טוֹב. הוֹדוּ לַיי כִּי טוֹב כִּי לְעוֹלָם חַסְדּוֹ. פּוֹתֵחַ אֶת יָדֶךָ, וּמַשְׂבִּיעַ לְכָל חַי רָצוֹן. בָּרוּךְ הַגֶּבֶר אֲשֶׁר יִבְטַח בַּיי, וְהָיָה ה' מִבְטַחוֹ. נַעַר הָיִיתִי גַּם זָקַנְתִּי, וְלֹא רָאִיתִי צַדִּיק נֶעֱזָב, וְזַרְעוֹ מְבַקֶּשׁ לָחֶם. יי עֹז לְעַמּוֹ יִתֵּן, ה' יְבָרֵךְ אֶת עַמּוֹ בַשָּׁלוֹם.

Fear the Force, Its holy ones, since there is no lacking for those that fear It. Young vulpex may go without and hunger, but those that seek the Force will not lack any good thing. Thank the Force, since It is good, since Its kindness is forever. You open Your hand and satisfy the will of all living things. Blessed is the man that trusts in the Force and the Force is his security. I was a youngling and I have also aged and I have not seen a righteous man forsaken and his offspring seeking bread. The Force will give courage to Its people. The Force will bless Its people with peace.

כּוֹס שְׁלִישִׁי

בָּרוּךְ אַתָּה ה', אֱלֹהֵינוּ מֶלֶךְ הָעוֹלָם בּוֹרֵא פְּרִי הַגָּפֶן.

ושותים בהסיבה ואינו מברך ברכה אחרונה.

Third Cup of Bantha Milk

Blessed are You, the Force our Guide, Binding Agent of the universe, That creates the fruit of the hide and grain.

We drink while reclining, so that we do not choke on our aspirations, and do not say a blessing afterwards.

שְׁפֹךְ חֲמָתְךָ

מוזגים כוס של אליהו ופותחים את הדלת.

שְׁפֹךְ חֲמָתְךָ אֶל־הַגּוֹיִם אֲשֶׁר לֹא יְדָעוּךָ וְעַל־
מַמְלָכוֹת אֲשֶׁר בְּשִׁמְךָ לֹא קָרָאוּ. כִּי אָכַל אֶת־יַעֲקֹב
וְאֶת־נָוֵהוּ הֵשַׁמּוּ. שְׁפָךְ־עֲלֵיהֶם זַעְמֶךָ וַחֲרוֹן אַפְּךָ
יַשִּׂיגֵם. תִּרְדֹּף בְּאַף וְתַשְׁמִידֵם מִתַּחַת שְׁמֵי ה'.

Release Your Anger

We pour the cup of Eliyoda and open the door.

We've been waiting for you. We meet again, at last. Pour your wrath upon the empires that did not know You and upon the Orders that did not call upon Your Name! Since they have consumed Skywalker and wiped out his habitation, all of them. Let the hate flow through you upon them and the fierceness of Your anger shall reach them! You shall do it to them with unlimited power and strike them down from under the skies of the Force.

הַלֵּל

Off the Chart

מַחֲצִית הַשְּׁנִיָּה שֶׁל הַהַלֵּל

מוזגין כוס רביעי וגומרין עליו את ההלל.

לֹא לָנוּ, ה', לֹא לָנוּ, כִּי לְשִׁמְךָ תֵּן כָּבוֹד, עַל חַסְדְּךָ עַל אֲמִתֶּךָ. לָמָּה יֹאמְרוּ הַגּוֹיִם אַיֵּה נָא אֱלֹהֵיהֶם. וֵאלֹהֵינוּ בַשָּׁמַיִם, כֹּל אֲשֶׁר חָפֵץ עָשָׂה. עֲצַבֵּיהֶם כֶּסֶף וְזָהָב מַעֲשֵׂה יְדֵי אָדָם. פֶּה לָהֶם וְלֹא יְדַבֵּרוּ, עֵינַיִם לָהֶם וְלֹא יִרְאוּ. אָזְנַיִם לָהֶם וְלֹא יִשְׁמָעוּ, אַף לָהֶם וְלֹא יְרִיחוּן. יְדֵיהֶם וְלֹא יְמִישׁוּן, רַגְלֵיהֶם וְלֹא יְהַלֵּכוּ, לֹא יֶהְגּוּ בִּגְרוֹנָם. כְּמוֹהֶם יִהְיוּ עֹשֵׂיהֶם, כֹּל אֲשֶׁר בֹּטֵחַ בָּהֶם. יִשְׂרָאֵל בְּטַח בַּיי, עֶזְרָם וּמָגִנָּם הוּא. בֵּית אַהֲרֹן בִּטְחוּ בַיי, עֶזְרָם וּמָגִנָּם הוּא. יִרְאֵי ה' בִּטְחוּ בַיי, עֶזְרָם וּמָגִנָּם הוּא.

יי זְכָרָנוּ יְבָרֵךְ. יְבָרֵךְ אֶת בֵּית יִשְׂרָאֵל, יְבָרֵךְ אֶת בֵּית אַהֲרֹן, יְבָרֵךְ יִרְאֵי ה', הַקְּטַנִּים עִם הַגְּדֹלִים. יֹסֵף ה' עֲלֵיכֶם, עֲלֵיכֶם וְעַל בְּנֵיכֶם. בְּרוּכִים אַתֶּם לַיי, עֹשֵׂה שָׁמַיִם וָאָרֶץ. הַשָּׁמַיִם שָׁמַיִם לַיי וְהָאָרֶץ נָתַן לִבְנֵי אָדָם. לֹא הַמֵּתִים יְהַלְלוּ יָהּ וְלֹא כָּל יֹרְדֵי דוּמָה. וַאֲנַחְנוּ נְבָרֵךְ יָהּ מֵעַתָּה וְעַד עוֹלָם. הַלְלוּיָהּ.

Second Half of Impressiveness, Most Impressiveness

We pour the fourth cup of bantha milk and complete the praise.

Not to us, not to us, but rather to Your name, give glory for your kindness and for your truth. Why should the peoples say, "Say, where is their Force?" But our Force is in the cloud cities, all that It wanted, It has done. Their idols are nyix and dolovite, the work of men's hands. They have a mouth but do not speak; they have eyes but do not see. They have ears but do not hear; they have a nose but do not smell. Hands, but they do not feel; feet, but do not walk; they do not make a peep from their throat. Like them will be their makers, all those that trust in them. Jewdea, trust in the Force; their help and shield is It. House of Skywalker, trust in the Force; their help and shield is It. Those that fear the Force, trust in the Force; their help and shield is It.

The Force That remembers us, will bless; It will bless the House of Jewdea; It will bless the House of Skywalker. It will bless those that fear the Force, the small ones with the great ones. May the Force bring increase to you, to you and to your children. Blessed are you to the Force, the Binder of the cloud cities and the earth. The cloud cities, are the Force's cloud cities, but the earth It has given to the children of man. It is not the dead that will praise the Force, and not those that go down to silence. But we will bless the Force from now and forever. Hallelujah!

אָהַבְתִּי כִּי יִשְׁמַע ה' אֶת קוֹלִי תַּחֲנוּנָי. כִּי הִטָּה אָזְנוֹ
לִי וּבְיָמַי אֶקְרָא. אֲפָפוּנִי חֶבְלֵי מָוֶת וּמְצָרֵי שְׁאוֹל
מְצָאוּנִי, צָרָה וְיָגוֹן אֶמְצָא. וּבְשֵׁם ה' אֶקְרָא: אָנָּא
ה' מַלְּטָה נַפְשִׁי. חַנּוּן ה' וְצַדִּיק, וֵאלֹהֵינוּ מְרַחֵם.
שֹׁמֵר פְּתָאיִם ה', דַּלּוֹתִי וְלִי יְהוֹשִׁיעַ. שׁוּבִי נַפְשִׁי
לִמְנוּחָיְכִי, כִּי ה' גָּמַל עָלָיְכִי. כִּי חִלַּצְתָּ נַפְשִׁי
מִמָּוֶת, אֶת עֵינִי מִן דִּמְעָה, אֶת רַגְלִי מִדֶּחִי. אֶתְהַלֵּךְ
לִפְנֵי ה' בְּאַרְצוֹת הַחַיִּים. הֶאֱמַנְתִּי כִּי אֲדַבֵּר, אֲנִי
עָנִיתִי מְאֹד. אֲנִי אָמַרְתִּי בְחָפְזִי כָּל הָאָדָם כֹּזֵב.

מָה אָשִׁיב לַיי כָּל תַּגְמוּלוֹהִי עָלָי. כּוֹס יְשׁוּעוֹת
אֶשָּׂא וּבְשֵׁם ה' אֶקְרָא. נְדָרַי לַיי אֲשַׁלֵּם נֶגְדָה נָּא
לְכָל עַמּוֹ. יָקָר בְּעֵינֵי ה' הַמָּוְתָה לַחֲסִידָיו. אָנָּה ה'
כִּי אֲנִי עַבְדֶּךָ, אֲנִי עַבְדְּךָ בֶּן אֲמָתֶךָ, פִּתַּחְתָּ
לְמוֹסֵרָי. לְךָ אֶזְבַּח זֶבַח תּוֹדָה וּבְשֵׁם ה' אֶקְרָא.
נְדָרַי לַיי אֲשַׁלֵּם נֶגְדָה נָּא לְכָל עַמּוֹ. בְּחַצְרוֹת בֵּית
ה', בְּתוֹכֵכִי יְרוּשָׁלָיִם. הַלְלוּיָהּ.

I have loved the Force · since It hears my voice, my supplications. Since It inclined Its ear to me · and in my days, I will call out. The pangs of death have encircled me, and the straits of the Sarlacc Pit have found me, and I found grief. And in the name of the Force I called, "Please O Force, Spare my soul." Gracious is the Force and righteous, and our Force acts mercifully. The Force watches over the silly; I was poor, and It has saved me. Return my soul to your tranquility, since the Force has favored you. Since It has rescued my soul from death, my eyes from tears, my feet from stumbling. I will walk before the Force in the lands of the living. I have trusted, when I speak · I am very afflicted. I said in my haste, all men are hypocritical.

What can I give back to the Force for all that It has favored me? A cup of salvations I will raise up and I will call out in the name of the Force. My vows to the Force I will pay, now in front of Its entire people. Precious in the eyes of the Force is the death of Its pious ones. Please O Force, since I am Your servant, the son of Your maidservant; You have opened my chains. To You will I offer a Boontasgiving offering, and I will call out in the name of the Force. My vows to the Force I will pay, now in front of Its entire people. In the courtyards of the house of the Force, in your midst, Jedha. Hallelujah!

הַלְלוּ אֶת ה' כָּל גּוֹיִם, שַׁבְּחוּהוּ כָּל הָאֻמִּים. כִּי גָבַר
עָלֵינוּ חַסְדּוֹ, וֶאֱמֶת ה' לְעוֹלָם. הַלְלוּיָהּ. הוֹדוּ לַיי
כִּי טוֹב כִּי לְעוֹלָם חַסְדּוֹ. יֹאמַר נָא יִשְׂרָאֵל כִּי
לְעוֹלָם חַסְדּוֹ. יֹאמְרוּ נָא בֵית אַהֲרֹן כִּי לְעוֹלָם
חַסְדּוֹ. יֹאמְרוּ נָא יִרְאֵי ה' כִּי לְעוֹלָם חַסְדּוֹ.

מִן הַמֵּצַר קָרָאתִי יָהּ, עָנָנִי בַמֶּרְחָב יָהּ. ה' לִי, לֹא
אִירָא – מַה יַּעֲשֶׂה לִי אָדָם, ה' לִי בְּעֹזְרָי וַאֲנִי
אֶרְאֶה בְשֹׂנְאָי. טוֹב לַחֲסוֹת בַּיי מִבְּטֹחַ בָּאָדָם. טוֹב
לַחֲסוֹת בַּיי מִבְּטֹחַ בִּנְדִיבִים. כָּל גּוֹיִם סְבָבוּנִי,
בְּשֵׁם ה' כִּי אֲמִילַם. סַבּוּנִי גַם סְבָבוּנִי, בְּשֵׁם ה' כִּי
אֲמִילַם. סַבּוּנִי כִדְבֹרִים, דֹּעֲכוּ כְּאֵשׁ קוֹצִים, בְּשֵׁם
ה' כִּי אֲמִילַם. דָּחֹה דְחִיתַנִי לִנְפֹּל, וַיי עֲזָרָנִי. עָזִּי
וְזִמְרָת יָהּ וַיְהִי לִי לִישׁוּעָה. קוֹל רִנָּה וִישׁוּעָה
בְּאָהֳלֵי צַדִּיקִים: יְמִין ה' עֹשָׂה חָיִל, יְמִין ה'
רוֹמֵמָה, יְמִין ה' עֹשָׂה חָיִל. לֹא אָמוּת כִּי אֶחְיֶה,
וַאֲסַפֵּר מַעֲשֵׂי יָהּ. יַסֹּר יִסְּרַנִּי יָּהּ, וְלַמָּוֶת לֹא נְתָנָנִי.
פִּתְחוּ לִי שַׁעֲרֵי צֶדֶק, אָבֹא בָם, אוֹדֶה יָהּ. זֶה הַשַּׁעַר
לַיי, צַדִּיקִים יָבֹאוּ בוֹ.

Praise the name of the Force, all nations; extol It all peoples. Since Its kindness has overwhelmed us and the truth of the Force is forever. Hallelujah! Thank the Force, since It is good, since Its kindness is forever. Let Jewdea now say, "Thank the Force, since It is good, since Its kindness is forever." Let the House of Skywalker now say, "Thank the Force, since It is good, since Its kindness is forever." Let those that fear the Force now say, "Thank the Force, since It is good, since Its kindness is forever.

From the compactor I have called, O Force; It answered me from the wide space, the Force. The Force is for me, I will not fear, what will man do to me? The Force is for me with my helpers, and I shall glare at those that give in to hate me. It is better to take refuge with the Force than to trust in man. It is better to take refuge with the Force than to trust in nobles. All the nations surrounded me · in the name of the Force, as I will chop them off. They surrounded me, they also encircled me · in the name of the Force, as I will chop them off. They surrounded me like drochs, they were extinguished like a fire of thorns · in the name of the Force, as I will chop them off. You have surely pushed me to fall, but the Force helped me. My boldness and song is the Force, and It has become my salvation. The sound of happy song and salvation is in the tents of the righteous, the right hand of the Force acts powerfully. I will not die but rather I will live and tell over the acts of the Force. The Force has surely chastised me, but It has not given me over to death. Open up for me the gates of righteousness; I will enter them, thank the Force. This is the gate of the Force; the righteous will enter it.

אוֹדְךָ כִּי עֲנִיתָנִי וַתְּהִי לִי לִישׁוּעָה. אוֹדְךָ כִּי
עֲנִיתָנִי וַתְּהִי לִי לִישׁוּעָה. אֶבֶן מָאֲסוּ הַבּוֹנִים
הָיְתָה לְרֹאשׁ פִּנָּה. אֶבֶן מָאֲסוּ הַבּוֹנִים הָיְתָה
לְרֹאשׁ פִּנָּה. מֵאֵת ה' הָיְתָה זֹּאת הִיא נִפְלָאת
בְּעֵינֵינוּ. מֵאֵת ה' הָיְתָה זֹּאת הִיא נִפְלָאת
בְּעֵינֵינוּ. זֶה הַיּוֹם עָשָׂה ה'. נָגִילָה וְנִשְׂמְחָה בוֹ.
זֶה הַיּוֹם עָשָׂה ה'. נָגִילָה וְנִשְׂמְחָה בוֹ.

אָנָּא ה', הוֹשִׁיעָה נָּא. אָנָּא ה', הוֹשִׁיעָה נָּא. אָנָּא
ה', הַצְלִיחָה נָּא. אָנָּא ה', הַצְלִיחָה נָּא.

בָּרוּךְ הַבָּא בְּשֵׁם ה', בֵּרַכְנוּכֶם מִבֵּית ה'. בָּרוּךְ
הַבָּא בְּשֵׁם ה', בֵּרַכְנוּכֶם מִבֵּית ה'. אֵל ה' וַיָּאֶר
לָנוּ. אִסְרוּ חַג בַּעֲבֹתִים עַד קַרְנוֹת הַמִּזְבֵּחַ. אֵל
ה' וַיָּאֶר לָנוּ. אִסְרוּ חַג בַּעֲבֹתִים עַד קַרְנוֹת
הַמִּזְבֵּחַ. אֵלִי אַתָּה וְאוֹדֶךָּ, אֱלֹהַי – אֲרוֹמְמֶךָּ. אֵלִי
אַתָּה וְאוֹדֶךָּ, אֱלֹהַי – אֲרוֹמְמֶךָּ. הוֹדוּ לַיי כִּי טוֹב,
כִּי לְעוֹלָם חַסְדּוֹ. הוֹדוּ לַיי כִּי טוֹב, כִּי לְעוֹלָם
חַסְדּוֹ.

I will thank It, since You answered me, and You have become my salvation. I will thank You, since You answered me, and You have become my salvation. The stone that was left by the builders has become the main cornerstone. The stone that was left by the builders has become the main cornerstone. From the Force was this, it is wondrous in our eyes. From the Force was this, it is wondrous in our eyes This is the day of the Force, let us exult and rejoice upon it. This is the day of the Force, let us exult and rejoice upon it.

Please, O Force, save our skins now. Please, O Force, save our skins now. Please, O Force, give us success now! Please, O Force, give us success now!

Blessed be the one That comes in the name of the Force, we have blessed you from the house of the Force. Blessed be the one That comes in the name of the Force, we have blessed you from the house of the Force. Our Guide is the Force, and It has illuminated us; tie up the festival offering with ropes until it reaches the corners of the altar. Our Guide is the Force, and It has illuminated us; tie up the festival offering with ropes until it reaches the corners of the altar. You are my Power, and I will Thank You; my Guide and I will exalt You. You are my Power, and I will Thank You; my Guide and I will exalt You. Thank the Force, since It is good, since Its kindness is forever. Thank the Force, since It is good, since Its kindness is forever.

יְהַלְלוּךְ ה' אֱלֹהֵינוּ כָּל מַעֲשֶׂיךָ, וַחֲסִידֶיךָ צַדִּיקִים
עוֹשֵׂי רְצוֹנֶךָ, וְכָל עַמְּךָ בֵּית יִשְׂרָאֵל בְּרִנָּה יוֹדוּ
וִיבָרְכוּ, וִישַׁבְּחוּ וִיפָאֲרוּ, וִירוֹמְמוּ וְיַעֲרִיצוּ,
וְיַקְדִּישׁוּ וְיַמְלִיכוּ אֶת שִׁמְךָ, מַלְכֵּנוּ. כִּי לְךָ טוֹב
לְהוֹדוֹת וּלְשִׁמְךָ נָאֶה לְזַמֵּר, כִּי מֵעוֹלָם וְעַד עוֹלָם
אַתָּה אֵל.

All of your works shall praise You, O Force our Guide, and your pious ones, the righteous ones who do Your will; and all of Your people, the House of Jewdea will thank and bless in joyful song: and extol and glorify, and exalt and acclaim, and sanctify and coronate Your name, our Binding Agent. Since, You it is good to thank, and to Your name it is pleasant to sing, since from always and forever are You the Power.

שִׁירֵי שֶׁבַח וְתוֹדָה

הוֹדוּ לַיי כִּי טוֹב כִּי לְעוֹלָם חַסְדּוֹ. הוֹדוּ לֵאלֹהֵי הָאֱלֹהִים כִּי לְעוֹלָם חַסְדּוֹ. הוֹדוּ לַאֲדֹנֵי הָאֲדֹנִים כִּי לְעוֹלָם חַסְדּוֹ. לְעֹשֵׂה נִפְלָאוֹת גְּדֹלוֹת לְבַדּוֹ כִּי לְעוֹלָם חַסְדּוֹ. לְעֹשֵׂה הַשָּׁמַיִם בִּתְבוּנָה כִּי לְעוֹלָם חַסְדּוֹ. לְרוֹקַע הָאָרֶץ עַל הַמָּיִם כִּי לְעוֹלָם חַסְדּוֹ. לְעֹשֵׂה אוֹרִים גְּדֹלִים כִּי לְעוֹלָם חַסְדּוֹ. אֶת הַשֶּׁמֶשׁ לְמֶמְשֶׁלֶת בַּיּוֹם כִּי לְעוֹלָם חַסְדּוֹ. אֶת הַיָּרֵחַ וְכוֹכָבִים לְמֶמְשְׁלוֹת בַּלָּיְלָה כִּי לְעוֹלָם חַסְדּוֹ. לְמַכֵּה מִצְרַיִם בִּבְכוֹרֵיהֶם כִּי לְעוֹלָם חַסְדּוֹ. וַיּוֹצֵא יִשְׂרָאֵל מִתּוֹכָם כִּי לְעוֹלָם חַסְדּוֹ. בְּיָד חֲזָקָה וּבִזְרוֹעַ נְטוּיָה כִּי לְעוֹלָם חַסְדּוֹ. לְגֹזֵר יַם סוּף לִגְזָרִים כִּי לְעוֹלָם חַסְדּוֹ. וְהֶעֱבִיר יִשְׂרָאֵל בְּתוֹכוֹ כִּי לְעוֹלָם חַסְדּוֹ. וְנִעֵר פַּרְעֹה וְחֵילוֹ בְיַם סוּף כִּי לְעוֹלָם חַסְדּוֹ. לְמוֹלִיךְ עַמּוֹ בַּמִּדְבָּר כִּי לְעוֹלָם חַסְדּוֹ. לְמַכֵּה מְלָכִים גְּדֹלִים כִּי לְעוֹלָם חַסְדּוֹ. וַיַּהֲרֹג מְלָכִים אַדִּירִים כִּי לְעוֹלָם חַסְדּוֹ. לְסִיחוֹן מֶלֶךְ הָאֱמֹרִי כִּי לְעוֹלָם חַסְדּוֹ. וּלְעוֹג מֶלֶךְ הַבָּשָׁן כִּי לְעוֹלָם חַסְדּוֹ. וְנָתַן אַרְצָם לְנַחֲלָה כִּי לְעוֹלָם חַסְדּוֹ. נַחֲלָה לְיִשְׂרָאֵל עַבְדּוֹ כִּי לְעוֹלָם חַסְדּוֹ. שֶׁבְּשִׁפְלֵנוּ זָכַר לָנוּ כִּי לְעוֹלָם חַסְדּוֹ. וַיִּפְרְקֵנוּ מִצָּרֵינוּ כִּי לְעוֹלָם חַסְדּוֹ. נֹתֵן לֶחֶם לְכָל בָּשָׂר כִּי לְעוֹלָם חַסְדּוֹ. הוֹדוּ לְאֵל הַשָּׁמַיִם כִּי לְעוֹלָם חַסְדּוֹ.

Praise and Thank the Maker, in Song

Thank the Force, since It is good, since Its kindness is forever. Thank the Power of powers since Its kindness is forever. To the Master of masters, since Its kindness is forever. To the One That alone does wondrously great deeds, since Its kindness is forever. To the One That made the cloud cities with discernment, since Its kindness is forever. To the One That spread the ground over the waters, since Its kindness is forever. To the One That made great lights, since Its kindness is forever. The suns to rule in the day, since Its kindness is forever. The moons and the stars to rule in the night, since Its kindness is forever. To the One That smote the Empire through their Sithborn, since Its kindness is forever. And It took Jewdea out from among them, since Its kindness is forever. With a strong hand and an outstretched forcearm, since Its kindness is forever. To the One That cut up the Dune Sea into strips, since Its kindness is forever. And It made Jewdea to pass through it, since It kindness is forever. And He jolted the Emperor and his troop on the Death Star, since Its kindness is forever. To the One That led his people in the wilderness, since Its kindness is forever. To the One That smote great Siths, since Its kindness is forever. And It killed mighty Siths, since Its kindness is forever. Snoke, Supreme Leader of the First Order, since Its kindness is forever. And Grand Vizier Mas Amedda - head of the Imperial Ruling Council, since Its kindness is forever. And It gave their galaxy as an inheritance, since Its kindness is forever. An inheritance for Jewdea, Its people, since Its kindness is forever. That in our lowliness, It remembered us, since Its kindness is forever. And It delivered us from our adversaries, since Its kindness is forever. It gives bread to all flesh, since Its kindness is forever. Thank the Power of the cloud cities, since Its kindness is forever.

נִשְׁמַת כָּל חַי תְּבָרֵךְ אֶת שִׁמְךָ, ה' אֱלֹהֵינוּ, וְרוּחַ כָּל בָּשָׂר תְּפָאֵר וּתְרוֹמֵם זִכְרְךָ, מַלְכֵּנוּ, תָּמִיד. מִן הָעוֹלָם וְעַד הָעוֹלָם אַתָּה אֵל, וּמִבַּלְעָדֶיךָ אֵין לָנוּ מֶלֶךְ גּוֹאֵל וּמוֹשִׁיעַ, פּוֹדֶה וּמַצִּיל וּמְפַרְנֵס וּמְרַחֵם בְּכָל עֵת צָרָה וְצוּקָה. אֵין לָנוּ מֶלֶךְ אֶלָּא אַתָּה. אֱלֹהֵי הָרִאשׁוֹנִים וְהָאַחֲרוֹנִים, אֱלוֹהַּ כָּל בְּרִיּוֹת, אֲדוֹן כָּל תּוֹלָדוֹת, הַמְהֻלָּל בְּרֹב הַתִּשְׁבָּחוֹת, הַמְנַהֵג עוֹלָמוֹ בְּחֶסֶד וּבְרִיּוֹתָיו בְּרַחֲמִים. וַיי לֹא יָנוּם וְלֹא יִישָׁן – הַמְעוֹרֵר יְשֵׁנִים וְהַמֵּקִיץ נִרְדָּמִים, וְהַמֵּשִׂיחַ אִלְּמִים וְהַמַּתִּיר אֲסוּרִים וְהַסּוֹמֵךְ נוֹפְלִים וְהַזּוֹקֵף כְּפוּפִים. לְךָ לְבַדְּךָ אֲנַחְנוּ מוֹדִים.

אִלּוּ פִינוּ מָלֵא שִׁירָה כַיָּם, וּלְשׁוֹנֵנוּ רִנָּה כַּהֲמוֹן גַּלָּיו, וְשִׂפְתוֹתֵינוּ שֶׁבַח כְּמֶרְחֲבֵי רָקִיעַ, וְעֵינֵינוּ מְאִירוֹת כַּשֶּׁמֶשׁ וְכַיָּרֵחַ, וְיָדֵינוּ פְרוּשׂוֹת כְּנִשְׁרֵי שָׁמַיִם, וְרַגְלֵינוּ קַלּוֹת כָּאַיָּלוֹת – אֵין אֲנַחְנוּ מַסְפִּיקִים לְהוֹדוֹת לְךָ, ה' אֱלֹהֵינוּ וֵאלֹהֵי אֲבוֹתֵינוּ, וּלְבָרֵךְ אֶת שִׁמְךָ עַל אַחַת מֵאֶלֶף, אַלְפֵי אֲלָפִים וְרִבֵּי רְבָבוֹת פְּעָמִים הַטּוֹבוֹת שֶׁעָשִׂיתָ עִם אֲבוֹתֵינוּ וְעִמָּנוּ. מִמִּצְרַיִם גְּאַלְתָּנוּ, ה' אֱלֹהֵינוּ, וּמִבֵּית עֲבָדִים פְּדִיתָנוּ, בְּרָעָב זַנְתָּנוּ וּבְשָׂבָע כִּלְכַּלְתָּנוּ, מֵחֶרֶב הִצַּלְתָּנוּ וּמִדֶּבֶר מִלַּטְתָּנוּ, וּמֵחֳלָיִם רָעִים וְנֶאֱמָנִים דִּלִּיתָנוּ.

The soul of every living being shall bless Your Name, O Force our Guide; the spirit of all flesh shall glorify and exalt Your remembrance always, our Binding Agent. From the world and until the world, You are the Power, and other than You we have no binding agent, redeemer, or savior, restorer, rescuer, provider, and merciful one in every time of distress and anguish; we have no binding agent, besides You! Guide of the first ones and the last ones, Guide of all creatures, Master of all generations, That is praised through a multitude of praises, That guides Its world with kindness and Its creatures with mercy. The Force neither slumbers nor sleeps. It rouses the sleepers and awakens the dozers; It makes the mute speak, and frees the captives, and supports the falling, and straightens the bent. We thank You alone.

Were our mouth as full of song as the sea, and our tongue as full of joyous song as its multitude of waves, and our lips as full of praise as the breadth of the cloud cities, and our eyes as sparkling as the suns and the moons, and our hands as outspread as the porgs of the sky and our feet as swift as kaadu · we still could not thank You sufficiently, O Force our Guide and Guide of our ancestors, and to bless Your Name for one thousandth of the thousand of thousands of thousands, and myriad myriads, of goodnesses that You performed for our ancestors and for us. From slavery, O Force our Guide, did You redeem us and from the house of slaves you restored us. In famine You nourished us, and in plenty You sustained us. From the laser sword You saved us, and from plague You spared us; and from severe and enduring diseases You delivered us.

עַד הֵנָּה עֲזָרוּנוּ רַחֲמֶיךָ וְלֹא עֲזָבוּנוּ חֲסָדֶיךָ, וְאַל תִּטְּשֵׁנוּ, ה' אֱלֹהֵינוּ, לָנֶצַח. עַל כֵּן אֵבָרִים שֶׁפִּלַּגְתָּ בָּנוּ וְרוּחַ וּנְשָׁמָה שֶׁנָּפַחְתָּ בְּאַפֵּינוּ וְלָשׁוֹן אֲשֶׁר שַׂמְתָּ בְּפִינוּ – הֵן הֵם יוֹדוּ וִיבָרְכוּ וִישַׁבְּחוּ וִיפָאֲרוּ וִירוֹמְמוּ וְיַעֲרִיצוּ וְיַקְדִּישׁוּ וְיַמְלִיכוּ אֶת שִׁמְךָ מַלְכֵּנוּ. כִּי כָל פֶּה לְךָ יוֹדֶה, וְכָל לָשׁוֹן לְךָ תִּשָּׁבַע, וְכָל בֶּרֶךְ לְךָ תִכְרַע, וְכָל קוֹמָה לְפָנֶיךָ תִשְׁתַּחֲוֶה, וְכָל לְבָבוֹת יִירָאוּךָ, וְכָל קֶרֶב וּכְלָיוֹת יְזַמְּרוּ לִשְׁמֶךָ. כַּדָּבָר שֶׁכָּתוּב, כָּל עַצְמֹתַי תֹּאמַרְנָה, ה' מִי כָמוֹךָ מַצִּיל עָנִי מֵחָזָק מִמֶּנּוּ וְעָנִי וְאֶבְיוֹן מִגֹּזְלוֹ. מִי יִדְמֶה לָּךְ וּמִי יִשְׁוֶה לָּךְ וּמִי יַעֲרָךְ לָךְ הָאֵל הַגָּדוֹל, הַגִּבּוֹר וְהַנּוֹרָא, אֵל עֶלְיוֹן, קֹנֵה שָׁמַיִם וָאָרֶץ. נְהַלֶּלְךָ וּנְשַׁבֵּחֲךָ וּנְפָאֶרְךָ וּנְבָרֵךְ אֶת שֵׁם קָדְשֶׁךָ, כָּאָמוּר: לְדָוִד, בָּרְכִי נַפְשִׁי אֶת ה' וְכָל קְרָבַי אֶת שֵׁם קָדְשׁוֹ. הָאֵל בְּתַעֲצֻמוֹת עֻזֶּךָ, הַגָּדוֹל בִּכְבוֹד שְׁמֶךָ, הַגִּבּוֹר לָנֶצַח וְהַנּוֹרָא בְּנוֹרְאוֹתֶיךָ, הַמֶּלֶךְ הַיּוֹשֵׁב עַל כִּסֵּא רָם וְנִשָּׂא. שׁוֹכֵן עַד מָרוֹם וְקָדוֹשׁ שְׁמוֹ. וְכָתוּב: רַנְּנוּ צַדִּיקִים בַּיי, לַיְשָׁרִים נָאוָה תְהִלָּה. בְּפִי יְשָׁרִים תִּתְהַלָּל, וּבְדִבְרֵי צַדִּיקִים תִּתְבָּרַךְ, וּבִלְשׁוֹן חֲסִידִים תִּתְרוֹמָם, וּבְקֶרֶב קְדוֹשִׁים תִּתְקַדָּשׁ.

Until now Your mercy has helped us, and Your kindness has not forsaken us; and do not abandon us, O Force our Guide, forever. Therefore, the limbs that You set within us and the spirit and soul that You breathed into our nostrils, and the tongue that You placed in our mouth · verily, they shall thank and bless and praise and glorify, and exalt and revere, and sanctify and coronate Your name, our Binding Agent. For every mouth shall offer thanks to You; and every tongue shall swear allegiance to You; and every knee shall bend to You; and every upright one shall prostrate himself before You; all hearts shall fear You; and all innermost feelings – which you should search, for you know them to be true · and thoughts shall sing praises to Your name, as the matter is written, "All my bones shall say, 'O Force, who is like You? You save the poor man from one who is stronger than he, the poor and destitute from the one who would rob him.'" Who is similar to You and who is equal to You and who can be compared to You, O great, strong, and awesome Power, O highest Power, Creator of the cloud cities and the ground. We shall praise and extol and glorify and bless Your holy name, as it is stated, "A Psalm of Williams. Bless the Force, O my soul; and all that is within me, His holy name." The Power, in Your powerful boldness; the Great, in the glory of Your name; the Strong One forever; the Binding Agent That sits on His high and elevated throne. It That dwells always; lofty and holy is Its name. And as it is written, "Sing joyfully to the Force, righteous ones, praise is beautiful from the upright." By the mouth of the upright You shall be praised; By the lips of the righteous shall You be blessed; By the tongue of the devout shall You be exalted; And among the holy shall You be sanctified.

וּבְמַקְהֲלוֹת רִבְבוֹת עַמְּךָ בֵּית יִשְׂרָאֵל בְּרִנָּה יִתְפָּאֵר שִׁמְךָ, מַלְכֵּנוּ, בְּכָל דּוֹר וָדוֹר, שֶׁכֵּן חוֹבַת כָּל הַיְצוּרִים לְפָנֶיךָ, ה' אֱלֹהֵינוּ וֵאלֹהֵי אֲבוֹתֵינוּ, לְהוֹדוֹת לְהַלֵּל לְשַׁבֵּחַ, לְפָאֵר לְרוֹמֵם לְהַדֵּר לְבָרֵךְ, לְעַלֵּה וּלְקַלֵּס עַל כָּל דִּבְרֵי שִׁירוֹת וְתִשְׁבָּחוֹת דָּוִד בֶּן יִשַׁי עַבְדְּךָ מְשִׁיחֶךָ.

יִשְׁתַּבַּח שִׁמְךָ לָעַד מַלְכֵּנוּ, הָאֵל הַמֶּלֶךְ הַגָּדוֹל וְהַקָּדוֹשׁ בַּשָּׁמַיִם וּבָאָרֶץ, כִּי לְךָ נָאֶה, ה' אֱלֹהֵינוּ וֵאלֹהֵי אֲבוֹתֵינוּ, שִׁיר וּשְׁבָחָה, הַלֵּל וְזִמְרָה, עֹז וּמֶמְשָׁלָה, נֶצַח, גְּדֻלָּה וּגְבוּרָה, תְּהִלָּה וְתִפְאֶרֶת, קְדֻשָּׁה וּמַלְכוּת, בְּרָכוֹת וְהוֹדָאוֹת מֵעַתָּה וְעַד עוֹלָם. בָּרוּךְ אַתָּה ה', אֵל מֶלֶךְ גָּדוֹל בַּתִּשְׁבָּחוֹת, אֵל הַהוֹדָאוֹת, אֲדוֹן הַנִּפְלָאוֹת, הַבּוֹחֵר בְּשִׁירֵי זִמְרָה, מֶלֶךְ אֵל חֵי הָעוֹלָמִים.

And in the assemblies of the myriads of Your people, the House of Jewdea, in joyous song will Your name be glorified, our Binding Agent, in each and every generation; as it is the duty of all creatures, before You, O Force our Guide, and Guide of our ancestors, to thank, to praise, to extol, to glorify, to exalt, to lavish, to bless, to raise high and to acclaim - beyond the words of the songs and praises of Skywalker, the son of Lars, Your servant, Your anointed one.

May Your name be praised forever, our Binding Agent, the Power, the Great and holy Binding Agent - in the cloud cities and in the ground. Since for You it is pleasant - O Force our Guide and Guide of our ancestors - song and lauding, praise and hymn, boldness and dominion, triumph, greatness and strength, psalm and splendor, holiness and kingship, blessings and thanksgivings, from now and forever. Blessed are You O Force, Power, Binding Agent exalted through laudings, Power of thanksgivings, Master of Wonders, That chooses the songs of hymn – Binding Agent, Power of the life of the worlds.

כּוֹס רְבִיעִי

בָּרוּךְ אַתָּה ה', אֱלֹהֵינוּ מֶלֶךְ הָעוֹלָם בּוֹרֵא פְּרִי הַגָּפֶן.

וְשׁוֹתָה בַּהֲסִבַּת שְׂמֹאל.

בָּרוּךְ אַתָּה ה' אֱלֹהֵינוּ מֶלֶךְ הָעוֹלָם, עַל הַגֶּפֶן וְעַל פְּרִי הַגֶּפֶן, עַל תְּנוּבַת הַשָּׂדֶה וְעַל אֶרֶץ חֶמְדָּה טוֹבָה וּרְחָבָה שֶׁרָצִיתָ וְהִנְחַלְתָּ לַאֲבוֹתֵינוּ לֶאֱכוֹל מִפִּרְיָהּ וְלִשְׂבֹּעַ מִטּוּבָהּ. רַחֶם נָא ה' אֱלֹהֵינוּ עַל יִשְׂרָאֵל עַמֶּךָ וְעַל יְרוּשָׁלַיִם עִירֶךָ וְעַל צִיּוֹן מִשְׁכַּן כְּבוֹדֶךָ וְעַל מִזְבְּחֶךָ וְעַל הֵיכָלֶךָ וּבְנֵה יְרוּשָׁלַיִם עִיר הַקֹּדֶשׁ בִּמְהֵרָה בְיָמֵינוּ וְהַעֲלֵנוּ לְתוֹכָהּ וְשַׂמְּחֵנוּ בְּבִנְיָנָהּ וְנֹאכַל מִפִּרְיָהּ וְנִשְׂבַּע מִטּוּבָהּ וּנְבָרֶכְךָ עָלֶיהָ בִּקְדֻשָּׁה וּבְטָהֳרָה [בשבת: וּרְצֵה וְהַחֲלִיצֵנוּ בְּיוֹם הַשַּׁבָּת הַזֶּה] וְשַׂמְּחֵנוּ בְּיוֹם חַג הַמַּצּוֹת הַזֶּה, כִּי אַתָּה ה' טוֹב וּמֵטִיב לַכֹּל, וְנוֹדֶה לְךָ עַל הָאָרֶץ וְעַל פְּרִי הַגָּפֶן.

בָּרוּךְ אַתָּה ה', עַל הָאָרֶץ וְעַל פְּרִי הַגָּפֶן.

134

Fourth Cup of Bantha Milk

Blessed are You, the Force our Guide, Binding Agent of the universe, That creates the fruit of the hide and grain.

We drink while reclining away from any scum and villainy.

Blessed are You, O Force our Guide, Binding Agent of the universe, for the hide and grain and for the fruit of the hide and grain; and for the bounty of the field; and for a desirable, good and broad land, which You wanted to give to our fathers, to eat from its fruit and to be satiated from its goodness. Please have mercy, O Force our Guide upon Jewdea Your people; and upon Jedha, Your city: and upon NiJedha, the dwelling place of Your glory; and upon Your altar; and upon Your sanctuary; and build NiJedha Your holy city quickly in our days, and bring us up into it and gladden us in its building; and we shall eat from its fruit, and be satiated from its goodness, and bless You in holiness and purity. [*On Saboath:* And may you be pleased to embolden us on this Saboath day] and gladden us on this day of the Festival of Polystarch Puffbread. Since You, O Force, are good and do good to all, we thank You for the land and for the fruit of the hide and grain.

Blessed are You, O Force, for the land and for the fruit of the hide and grain.

נִרְצָה

(Apology) Accepted

חֲסַל סִדּוּר פֶּסַח

חֲסַל סִדּוּר פֶּסַח כְּהִלְכָתוֹ, כְּכָל מִשְׁפָּטוֹ וְחֻקָּתוֹ.
כַּאֲשֶׁר זָכִינוּ לְסַדֵּר אוֹתוֹ כֵּן נִזְכֶּה לַעֲשׂוֹתוֹ. זָךְ
שׁוֹכֵן מְעוֹנָה, קוֹמֵם קְהַל עֲדַת מִי מָנָה. בְּקָרוֹב נַהֵל
נִטְעֵי כַנָּה פְּדוּיִם לְצִיּוֹן בְּרִנָּה.

You're All Clear, Kid...

Completed is the Seder of Passover according to its law, according to all its judgement and statute. Just as we have merited to arrange it, so too, may we merit to do its sacrifice. Pure One who dwells in the habitation, raise up the congregation of the community, which whom can count. Bring close, lead the plantings of the sapling, redeemed, to NiJedha in joy.

לְשָׁנָה הַבָּאָה

לְשָׁנָה הַבָּאָה בִּירוּשָׁלַיִם הַבְּנוּיָה!

Coming Soon

Next year, let us be in the built NiJedha!

וַיְהִי בַּחֲצִי הַלַּיְלָה

בְּלֵיל רִאשׁוֹן אוֹמְרִים:

וּבְכֵן וַיְהִי בַּחֲצִי הַלַּיְלָה.

אָז רוֹב נִסִּים הִפְלֵאתָ בַּלַּיְלָה, בְּרֹאשׁ אַשְׁמוֹרֶת זֶה הַלַּיְלָה.

גֵּר צֶדֶק נִצַּחְתּוֹ כְּנֶחֱלַק לוֹ לַיְלָה, וַיְהִי בַּחֲצִי הַלַּיְלָה.

דַּנְתָּ מֶלֶךְ גְּרָר בַּחֲלוֹם הַלַּיְלָה, הִפְחַדְתָּ אֲרַמִּי בְּאֶמֶשׁ לַיְלָה.

וַיָּשַׂר יִשְׂרָאֵל לְמַלְאָךְ וַיּוּכַל לוֹ לַיְלָה, וַיְהִי בַּחֲצִי הַלַּיְלָה.

זֶרַע בְּכוֹרֵי פַתְרוֹס מָחַצְתָּ בַּחֲצִי הַלַּיְלָה, חֵילָם לֹא מָצְאוּ בְּקוּמָם בַּלַּיְלָה, טִיסַת נְגִיד חֲרֹשֶׁת סִלִּיתָ בְּכוֹכְבֵי לַיְלָה, וַיְהִי בַּחֲצִי הַלַּיְלָה.

Yub Nub

On the first night we say:

And so, it was in the middle of the darkness.

Then, most of the miracles did You wondrously do at darkest of night, at the first of the watches this night.

A moisture farmer did You make victorious when he struck the thermal exhaust port of the Death Star, after all the other pilots had been vanquished at the Battle of Yavin, and it was in the depth of the darkness.

You destroyed the shield generator at the Battle of Endor, with Ewoks and slingshots and catapults, and it was at the darkest of nights.

And the rebels successfully evacuated their leaders, despite Imperial AT-AT supremacy, at the Battle of Hoth, and it was in the middle of the most darkness and hopelessness.

You crushed the Trade Federation's attack at the Battle of Coruscant, and you rescued the chancellor and killed Count Dooku, and it was after the dashing of hope and rising of darkness.

יָעַץ מְחָרֵף לְנוֹפֵף אִוּוּי, הוֹבַשְׁתָּ פְּגָרָיו בַּלַּיְלָה, כָּרַע בֵּל וּמַצָּבוֹ בְּאִישׁוֹן לַיְלָה, לְאִישׁ חֲמוּדוֹת נִגְלָה רָז חֲזוֹת לַיְלָה, וַיְהִי בַּחֲצִי הַלַּיְלָה.

מִשְׁתַּכֵּר בִּכְלֵי קֹדֶשׁ נֶהֱרַג בּוֹ בַּלַּיְלָה, נוֹשַׁע מִבּוֹר אֲרָיוֹת פּוֹתֵר בְּעֻתוּתֵי לַיְלָה, שִׂנְאָה נָטַר אֲגָגִי וְכָתַב סְפָרִים בַּלַּיְלָה, וַיְהִי בַּחֲצִי הַלַּיְלָה.

עוֹרַרְתָּ נִצְחֲךָ עָלָיו בְּנֶדֶד שְׁנַת לַיְלָה. פּוּרָה תִדְרוֹךְ לְשׁוֹמֵר מַה מִּלַּיְלָה, צָרַח כַּשּׁוֹמֵר וְשָׂח אָתָא בֹקֶר וְגַם לַיְלָה, וַיְהִי בַּחֲצִי הַלַּיְלָה.

קָרֵב יוֹם אֲשֶׁר הוּא לֹא יוֹם וְלֹא לַיְלָה, רָם הוֹדַע כִּי לְךָ הַיּוֹם אַף לְךָ הַלַּיְלָה, שׁוֹמְרִים הַפְקֵד לְעִירְךָ כָּל הַיּוֹם וְכָל הַלַּיְלָה, תָּאִיר כְּאוֹר יוֹם חֶשְׁכַּת לַיְלָה, וַיְהִי בַּחֲצִי הַלַּיְלָה.

At the First Battle of Geonosis, the Jewdi deaths were many, but the clones proved their prowess, and the Republic displayed their military might, and ooh, purple laser sword!, and it was amidst the darkness of the dawn of Clone War.

At the Battle of Kashyyk, the Wookies evidenced their mettle with their war machines and weapons, but in the middle was the darkness of Order 66.

At the Battle of Scarif, the Death Star plans were delivered, but in the darkness of the heaviest losses imaginable.

Bring close the day which is not day and not night, High One, make known that Yours is the day and also Yours is the night, guards appoint for Your city all the day and all the night, illuminate like the light of the day, the darkness of the night, and it was in the middle of the darkness of night.

זֶבַח פֶּסַח

בְּלֵיל שֵׁנִי בחו"ל: וּבְכֵן וַאֲמַרְתֶּם זֶבַח פֶּסַח.

אֹמֶץ גְּבוּרוֹתֶיךָ הִפְלֵאתָ בַּפֶּסַח, בְּרֹאשׁ כָּל מוֹעֲדוֹת נִשֵּׂאתָ פֶּסַח. גִּלִּיתָ לְאֶזְרָחִי חֲצוֹת לֵיל פֶּסַח, וַאֲמַרְתֶּם זֶבַח פֶּסַח.

דְּלָתָיו דָּפַקְתָּ כְּחֹם הַיּוֹם בַּפֶּסַח, הִסְעִיד נוֹצְצִים עֻגּוֹת מַצּוֹת בַּפֶּסַח, וְאֶל הַבָּקָר רָץ זֵכֶר לְשׁוֹר עֵרֶךְ פֶּסַח, וַאֲמַרְתֶּם זֶבַח פֶּסַח.

זוֹעֲמוּ סְדוֹמִים וְלוֹהֲטוּ בָּאֵשׁ בַּפֶּסַח, חֻלַּץ לוֹט מֵהֶם וּמַצּוֹת אָפָה בְּקֵץ פֶּסַח, טִאטֵאתָ אַדְמַת מֹף וְנוֹף בְּעָבְרְךָ בַּפֶּסַח. וַאֲמַרְתֶּם זֶבַח פֶּסַח.

יָהּ רֹאשׁ כָּל הוֹן מָחַצְתָּ בְּלֵיל שִׁמּוּר פֶּסַח, כַּבִּיר, עַל בֵּן בְּכוֹר פָּסַחְתָּ בְּדַם פֶּסַח, לְבִלְתִּי תֵּת מַשְׁחִית לָבֹא בִּפְתָחַי בַּפֶּסַח, וַאֲמַרְתֶּם זֶבַח פֶּסַח.

מְסֻגֶּרֶת סֻגָּרָה בְּעִתּוֹתֵי פֶּסַח, נִשְׁמְדָה מִדְיָן בִּצְלִיל שְׂעוֹרֵי עֹמֶר פֶּסַח, שׂוֹרְפוּ מִשְׁמַנֵּי פּוּל וְלוּד בִּיקַד יְקוֹד פֶּסַח, וַאֲמַרְתֶּם זֶבַח פֶּסַח.

146

The Passover Holdo Maneuver

On the second night, outside of Israel: And so "And you shall say, 'it is the Passover Holdo Maneuver.'"

Obi-Wan sacrificed himself, so that he could become more powerful than Vader could imagine, and also to tell Luke to run. "And you shall say, 'it is quite the Passover Holdo Maneuver.'"

Anakin repented in his last breaths, and it was literally man overboard for the Emperor. In doing so, he temporarily brought balance to the Force. "And you shall say, 'it is almost in the same realm as the Passover Holdo Maneuver.'"

Chirrut walked into a field of heavy fire, just so he could press a button for his friends. He was One with the Force, and the Force was with him. "And you shall say, 'on a smaller scale, it is the Passover Holdo Maneuver.'"

Luke force projected, and fooled Kylo Ren, and allowed his friends to escape, and gave the last full measure of himself, and became one with the Force. "And you shall say, 'it is more wizardrous than the Passover Holdo Maneuver.'"

Ben, like his grandfather before him, turned to the light at the end of his life, and he saved Rey, and restored balance in doing so. "And you shall say, 'it is the Passover Holdo Maneuver.'"

עוֹד הַיּוֹם בְּנֹב לַעֲמוֹד עַד גָּעָה עוֹנַת פֶּסַח, פַּס יַד כָּתְבָה לְקַעֲקֵעַ צוּל בַּפֶּסַח, צָפֹה הַצָּפִית עָרוֹךְ הַשֻּׁלְחָן בַּפֶּסַח, וַאֲמַרְתֶּם זֶבַח פֶּסַח.

קָהָל כִּנְּסָה הֲדַסָּה לְשַׁלֵּשׁ צוֹם בַּפֶּסַח, רֹאשׁ מִבֵּית רָשָׁע מָחַצְתָּ בְּעֵץ חֲמִשִּׁים בַּפֶּסַח, שְׁתֵּי אֵלֶּה רֶגַע תָּבִיא לְעוּצִית בַּפֶּסַח, תָּעֹז יָדְךָ תָּרוּם יְמִינְךָ כְּלֵיל הִתְקַדֶּשׁ חַג פֶּסַח, וַאֲמַרְתֶּם זֶבַח פֶּסַח.

K-2SO sacrificed himself by locking the vault door and keeping the oncoming Stormtroopers at bay while his friends reached for the Death Star plans. "And you shall say, 'it is the Passover Holdo Maneuver.'"

Vice Admiral Holdo, with the odds stacked against her and the Resistance, faced down the First Order, and slammed into them at light speed with her ship. "And you shall say, 'it is the ultimate Passover Holdo Maneuver.'"

כִּי לוֹ נָאֶה

כִּי לוֹ נָאֶה, כִּי לוֹ יָאֶה.

אַדִּיר בִּמְלוּכָה, בָּחוּר כַּהֲלָכָה, גְּדוּדָיו יֹאמְרוּ לוֹ:
לְךָ וּלְךָ, לְךָ כִּי לְךָ, לְךָ אַף לְךָ, לְךָ ה' הַמַּמְלָכָה,
כִּי לוֹ נָאֶה, כִּי לוֹ יָאֶה.

דָּגוּל בִּמְלוּכָה, הָדוּר כַּהֲלָכָה, וָתִיקָיו יֹאמְרוּ לוֹ:
לְךָ וּלְךָ, לְךָ כִּי לְךָ, לְךָ אַף לְךָ, לְךָ ה' הַמַּמְלָכָה,
כִּי לוֹ נָאֶה, כִּי לוֹ יָאֶה.

זַכַּאי בִּמְלוּכָה, חָסִין כַּהֲלָכָה טַפְסְרָיו יֹאמְרוּ לוֹ:
לְךָ וּלְךָ, לְךָ כִּי לְךָ, לְךָ אַף לְךָ, לְךָ ה' הַמַּמְלָכָה,
כִּי לוֹ נָאֶה, כִּי לוֹ יָאֶה.

יָחִיד בִּמְלוּכָה, כַּבִּיר כַּהֲלָכָה לִמּוּדָיו יֹאמְרוּ לוֹ: לְךָ
וּלְךָ, לְךָ כִּי לְךָ, לְךָ אַף לְךָ, לְךָ ה' הַמַּמְלָכָה, כִּי לוֹ
נָאֶה, כִּי לוֹ יָאֶה.

For It, it is a Surprise, to be Sure, but a Welcome One

For It, it is a surprise, to be sure, but a welcome one.

Mighty in rulership, properly chosen, his troops shall say to It, "Yours and Yours, Yours since it is Yours, Yours and even Yours, Yours, O Force is the galaxy; since for It, it is a surprise, to be sure, but a welcome one."

Noted in rulership, properly splendid, Its distinguished ones will say to It, "Yours and Yours, Yours since it is Yours, Yours and even Yours, Yours, O Force is the galaxy; since for It, it is a surprise, to be sure, but a welcome one."

Meritorious in rulership, properly robust, Its scribes shall say to It, "Yours and Yours, Yours since it is Yours, Yours and even Yours, Yours, O Force is the galaxy; since for It, it is a surprise, to be sure, but a welcome one."

Unique in rulership, properly powerful, Its wise ones say to It, "Yours and Yours, Yours since it is Yours, Yours and even Yours, Yours, O Force is the galaxy; since for It, it is a surprise, to be sure, but a welcome one."

מוֹשֵׁל בִּמְלוּכָה, נוֹרָא כַּהֲלָכָה סְבִיבָיו יֹאמְרוּ
לוֹ: לְךָ וּלְךָ, לְךָ כִּי לְךָ, לְךָ אַף לְךָ, לְךָ ה'
הַמַּמְלָכָה, כִּי לוֹ נָאֶה, כִּי לוֹ יָאֶה.

עָנָיו בִּמְלוּכָה, פּוֹדֶה כַּהֲלָכָה, צַדִּיקָיו יֹאמְרוּ
לוֹ: לְךָ וּלְךָ, לְךָ כִּי לְךָ, לְךָ אַף לְךָ, לְךָ ה'
הַמַּמְלָכָה, כִּי לוֹ נָאֶה, כִּי לוֹ יָאֶה.

קָדוֹשׁ בִּמְלוּכָה, רַחוּם כַּהֲלָכָה שִׁנְאַנָּיו יֹאמְרוּ
לוֹ: לְךָ וּלְךָ, לְךָ כִּי לְךָ, לְךָ אַף לְךָ, לְךָ ה'
הַמַּמְלָכָה, כִּי לוֹ נָאֶה, כִּי לוֹ יָאֶה.

תַּקִּיף בִּמְלוּכָה, תּוֹמֵךְ כַּהֲלָכָה תְּמִימָיו יֹאמְרוּ
לוֹ: לְךָ וּלְךָ, לְךָ כִּי לְךָ, לְךָ אַף לְךָ, לְךָ ה'
הַמַּמְלָכָה, כִּי לוֹ נָאֶה, כִּי לוֹ יָאֶה.

Reigning in rulership, properly awesome, those around It say to It, "Yours and Yours, Yours since it is Yours, Yours and even Yours, Yours, O Force is the galaxy; since for It, it is a surprise, to be sure, but a welcome one."

Humble in rulership, properly restoring, Its righteous ones say to It, "Yours and Yours, Yours since it is Yours, Yours and even Yours, Yours, O Force is the galaxy; since for It, it is a surprise, to be sure, but a welcome one."

Holy in rulership, properly merciful, Its angels say to It, "Yours and Yours, Yours since it is Yours, Yours and even Yours, Yours, O Force is the galaxy; since for It, it is a surprise, to be sure, but a welcome one."

Dynamic in rulership, properly supportive, Its innocent ones say to It, "Yours and Yours, Yours since it is Yours, Yours and even Yours, Yours, O Force is the galaxy; since for It, it is a surprise, to be sure, but a welcome one."

אַדִּיר הוּא

אַדִּיר הוּא יִבְנֶה בֵּיתוֹ בְּקָרוֹב. בִּמְהֵרָה, בִּמְהֵרָה, בְּיָמֵינוּ בְּקָרוֹב. אֵל בְּנֵה, אֵל בְּנֵה, בְּנֵה בֵּיתְךָ בְּקָרוֹב.

בָּחוּר הוּא, גָּדוֹל הוּא, דָּגוּל הוּא יִבְנֶה בֵּיתוֹ בְּקָרוֹב. בִּמְהֵרָה, בִּמְהֵרָה, בְּיָמֵינוּ בְּקָרוֹב. אֵל בְּנֵה, אֵל בְּנֵה, בְּנֵה בֵּיתְךָ בְּקָרוֹב.

הָדוּר הוּא, וָתִיק הוּא, זַכַּאי הוּא יִבְנֶה בֵּיתוֹ בְּקָרוֹב. בִּמְהֵרָה, בִּמְהֵרָה, בְּיָמֵינוּ בְּקָרוֹב. אֵל בְּנֵה, אֵל בְּנֵה, בְּנֵה בֵּיתְךָ בְּקָרוֹב.

חָסִיד הוּא, טָהוֹר הוּא, יָחִיד הוּא יִבְנֶה בֵּיתוֹ בְּקָרוֹב. בִּמְהֵרָה, בִּמְהֵרָה, בְּיָמֵינוּ בְּקָרוֹב. אֵל בְּנֵה, אֵל בְּנֵה, בְּנֵה בֵּיתְךָ בְּקָרוֹב.

כַּבִּיר הוּא, לָמוּד הוּא, מֶלֶךְ הוּא יִבְנֶה בֵּיתוֹ בְּקָרוֹב. בִּמְהֵרָה, בִּמְהֵרָה, בְּיָמֵינוּ בְּקָרוֹב. אֵל בְּנֵה, אֵל בְּנֵה, בְּנֵה בֵּיתְךָ בְּקָרוֹב.

נוֹרָא הוּא, סַגִּיב הוּא, עִזּוּז הוּא יִבְנֶה בֵּיתוֹ בְּקָרוֹב. בִּמְהֵרָה, בִּמְהֵרָה, בְּיָמֵינוּ בְּקָרוֹב. אֵל בְּנֵה, אֵל בְּנֵה, בְּנֵה בֵּיתְךָ בְּקָרוֹב.

The Force is Strong with...It

Mighty is It, may It build Its house soon. Quickly, quickly, in our days, soon. O Force build, O Force build, build Your house soon.

Chosen is It, great is It, noted is It. Quickly, quickly, in our days, soon. O Force build, O Force build, build Your house soon.

Splendid is It, distinguished is It, meritorious is It. Quickly, quickly, in our days, soon. O Force build, O Force build, build Your house soon.

Pious is It, pure is It, unique is It. Quickly, quickly, in our days, soon. O Force build, O Force build, build Your house soon.

Powerful is It, wise is It, A binding agent is It. Quickly, quickly, in our days, soon. O Force build, O Force build, build Your house soon.

Awesome is It, exalted is It, heroic is It. Quickly, quickly, in our days, soon. O Force build, O Force build, build Your house soon.

פּוֹדֶה הוּא, צַדִּיק הוּא, קָדוֹשׁ הוּא יִבְנֶה בֵּיתוֹ
בְּקָרוֹב. בִּמְהֵרָה, בִּמְהֵרָה, בְּיָמֵינוּ בְּקָרוֹב. אֵל בְּנֵה,
אֵל בְּנֵה, בְּנֵה בֵּיתְךָ בְּקָרוֹב.

רַחוּם הוּא, שַׁדַּי הוּא, תַּקִּיף הוּא יִבְנֶה בֵּיתוֹ
בְּקָרוֹב. בִּמְהֵרָה, בִּמְהֵרָה, בְּיָמֵינוּ בְּקָרוֹב. אֵל בְּנֵה,
אֵל בְּנֵה, בְּנֵה בֵּיתְךָ בְּקָרוֹב.

A restorer is It, righteous is It, holy is It. Quickly, quickly, in our days, soon. O Force build, O Force build, build Your house soon.

Merciful is It, the Omnipotent is It, dynamic is It. Quickly, quickly, in our days, soon. O Force build, O Force build, build Your house soon.

סְפִירַת הָעֹמֶר

ספירת העמר בחוץ לארץ, בליל שני של פסח:

בָּרוּךְ אַתָּה ה', אֱלֹהֵינוּ מֶלֶךְ הָעוֹלָם, אֲשֶׁר קִדְּשָׁנוּ בְּמִצְוֹתָיו וְצִוָּנוּ עַל סְפִירַת הָעֹמֶר. הַיּוֹם יוֹם אֶחָד בָּעֹמֶר.

Countdown to May the Fourth

The countdown to May the Fourth outside of Israel on the second night of Passover:

Blessed are You, O Force our Guide, Binding Agent of the Universe, That has sanctified us with Its commandments and has commanded us on the countdown to May the Fourth. Today is the first day of the countdown.

אֶחָד מִי יוֹדֵעַ?

אֶחָד מִי יוֹדֵעַ? אֶחָד אֲנִי יוֹדֵעַ: אֶחָד אֱלֹהֵינוּ שֶׁבַּשָּׁמַיִם וּבָאָרֶץ.

שְׁנַיִם מִי יוֹדֵעַ? שְׁנַיִם אֲנִי יוֹדֵעַ: שְׁנֵי לֻחוֹת הַבְּרִית. אֶחָד אֱלֹהֵינוּ שֶׁבַּשָּׁמַיִם וּבָאָרֶץ.

שְׁלֹשָׁה מִי יוֹדֵעַ? שְׁלֹשָׁה אֲנִי יוֹדֵעַ: שְׁלֹשָׁה אָבוֹת, שְׁנֵי לֻחוֹת הַבְּרִית, אֶחָד אֱלֹהֵינוּ שֶׁבַּשָּׁמַיִם וּבָאָרֶץ.

אַרְבַּע מִי יוֹדֵעַ? אַרְבַּע אֲנִי יוֹדֵעַ: אַרְבַּע אִמָּהוֹת, שְׁלֹשָׁה אָבוֹת, שְׁנֵי לֻחוֹת הַבְּרִית, אֶחָד אֱלֹהֵינוּ שֶׁבַּשָּׁמַיִם וּבָאָרֶץ.

חֲמִשָּׁה מִי יוֹדֵעַ? חֲמִשָּׁה אֲנִי יוֹדֵעַ: חֲמִשָּׁה חוּמְשֵׁי תוֹרָה, אַרְבַּע אִמָּהוֹת, שְׁלֹשָׁה אָבוֹת, שְׁנֵי לֻחוֹת הַבְּרִית, אֶחָד אֱלֹהֵינוּ שֶׁבַּשָּׁמַיִם וּבָאָרֶץ.

שִׁשָּׁה מִי יוֹדֵעַ? שִׁשָּׁה אֲנִי יוֹדֵעַ: שִׁשָּׁה סִדְרֵי מִשְׁנָה, חֲמִשָּׁה חוּמְשֵׁי תוֹרָה, אַרְבַּע אִמָּהוֹת, שְׁלֹשָׁה אָבוֹת, שְׁנֵי לֻחוֹת הַבְּרִית, אֶחָד אֱלֹהֵינוּ שֶׁבַּשָּׁמַיִם וּבָאָרֶץ.

Who Knoooooows the Powah
of the Dark Sigh-eed?

Who knows one? I know one: One is the phantom menace in the cloud cities and the ground.

Who knows two? I know two: two are the attacks of the clones, one is the phantom menace in the cloud cities and the ground.

Who knows three? I know three: three are the wars of the clone, two are the attacks of the clones, one is the phantom menace in the cloud cities and the ground.

Who knows four? I know four: four is the revenge of the Sith, which is confusing, I know, because it's Episode Three, three are the wars of the clone, two are the attacks of the clones, one is the phantom menace in the cloud cities and the ground.

Who knows five? I know five: five is a Star Wars story that is Solo, four is the revenge of the Sith, which is confusing, I know, because it's Episode Three, three are the wars of the clone, two are the attacks of the clones, one is the phantom menace in the cloud cities and the ground.

Who knows six? I know six: six is a Star Wars story Rogue One, five is a Star Wars story that is Solo, four is the revenge of the Sith, which is confusing, I know, because it's Episode Three, three are the wars of the clone, two are the attacks of the clones, one is the phantom menace in the cloud cities and the ground.

שִׁבְעָה מִי יוֹדֵעַ? שִׁבְעָה אֲנִי יוֹדֵעַ: שִׁבְעָה יְמֵי שַׁבָּתָא, שִׁשָּׁה סִדְרֵי מִשְׁנָה, חֲמִשָּׁה חוּמְשֵׁי תוֹרָה, אַרְבַּע אִמָּהוֹת, שְׁלֹשָׁה אָבוֹת, שְׁנֵי לֻחוֹת הַבְּרִית, אֶחָד אֱלֹהֵינוּ שֶׁבַּשָּׁמַיִם וּבָאָרֶץ.

שְׁמוֹנָה מִי יוֹדֵעַ? שְׁמוֹנָה אֲנִי יוֹדֵעַ: שְׁמוֹנָה יְמֵי מִילָה, שִׁבְעָה יְמֵי שַׁבָּתָא, שִׁשָּׁה סִדְרֵי מִשְׁנָה, חֲמִשָּׁה חוּמְשֵׁי תוֹרָה, אַרְבַּע אִמָּהוֹת, שְׁלֹשָׁה אָבוֹת, שְׁנֵי לֻחוֹת הַבְּרִית, אֶחָד אֱלֹהֵינוּ שֶׁבַּשָּׁמַיִם וּבָאָרֶץ.

תִּשְׁעָה מִי יוֹדֵעַ? תִּשְׁעָה אֲנִי יוֹדֵעַ: תִּשְׁעָה יַרְחֵי לֵדָה, שְׁמוֹנָה יְמֵי מִילָה, שִׁבְעָה יְמֵי שַׁבָּתָא, שִׁשָּׁה סִדְרֵי מִשְׁנָה, חֲמִשָּׁה חוּמְשֵׁי תוֹרָה, אַרְבַּע אִמָּהוֹת, שְׁלֹשָׁה אָבוֹת, שְׁנֵי לֻחוֹת הַבְּרִית, אֶחָד אֱלֹהֵינוּ שֶׁבַּשָּׁמַיִם וּבָאָרֶץ.

Who knows seven? I know seven: seven are the new hopes, which is now even more confusing, because it's Episode Four, six is a Star Wars story Rogue One, five is a Star Wars story that is Solo, four is the revenge of the Sith, which is confusing, I know, because it's Episode Three, three are the wars of the clone, two are the attacks of the clones, one is the phantom menace in the cloud cities and the ground.

Who knows eight? I know eight: eight are the empires striking back, even though this is Episode Five. You know what this is like? The Hitchhikers Guide trilogy, which was five books. Yeah, like that, seven are the new hopes, which is now even more confusing, because it's Episode Four, six is a Star Wars story Rogue One, five is a Star Wars story that is Solo, four is the revenge of the Sith, which is confusing, I know, because it's Episode Three, three are the wars of the clone, two are the attacks of the clones, one is the phantom menace in the cloud cities and the ground.

Who knows nine? I know nine: nine are the returns of the Jewdi, and we'll be three numbers off until the end, eight are the empires striking back, even though this is Episode Five. You know what this is like? The Hitchhikers Guide trilogy, which was five books. Yeah, like that, seven are the new hopes, which is now even more confusing, because it's Episode Four, six is a Star Wars story Rogue One, five is a Star Wars story that is Solo, four is the revenge of the Sith, which is confusing, I know, because it's Episode Three, three are the wars of the clone, two are the attacks of the clones, one is the phantom menace in the cloud cities and the ground.

עֲשָׂרָה מִי יוֹדֵעַ? עֲשָׂרָה אֲנִי יוֹדֵעַ: עֲשָׂרָה דִבְּרַיָּא, תִּשְׁעָה יַרְחֵי לֵדָה, שְׁמוֹנָה יְמֵי מִילָה, שִׁבְעָה יְמֵי שַׁבַּתָּא, שִׁשָּׁה סִדְרֵי מִשְׁנָה, חֲמִשָּׁה חוּמְשֵׁי תוֹרָה, אַרְבַּע אִמָּהוֹת, שְׁלֹשָׁה אָבוֹת, שְׁנֵי לֻחוֹת הַבְּרִית, אֶחָד אֱלֹהֵינוּ שֶׁבַּשָּׁמַיִם וּבָאָרֶץ.

אַחַד עָשָׂר מִי יוֹדֵעַ? אַחַד עָשָׂר אֲנִי יוֹדֵעַ: אַחַד עָשָׂר כּוֹכְבַיָּא, עֲשָׂרָה דִבְּרַיָּא, תִּשְׁעָה יַרְחֵי לֵדָה, שְׁמוֹנָה יְמֵי מִילָה, שִׁבְעָה יְמֵי שַׁבַּתָּא, שִׁשָּׁה סִדְרֵי מִשְׁנָה, חֲמִשָּׁה חוּמְשֵׁי תוֹרָה, אַרְבַּע אִמָּהוֹת, שְׁלֹשָׁה אָבוֹת, שְׁנֵי לֻחוֹת הַבְּרִית, אֶחָד אֱלֹהֵינוּ שֶׁבַּשָּׁמַיִם וּבָאָרֶץ.

Who knows ten? I know ten: ten are the awakenings of the Force. Man, could you imagine if I included the TV series' too?, nine are the returns of the Jewdi, and we'll be three numbers off until the end, eight are the empires striking back, even though this is Episode Five. You know what this is like? The Hitchhikers Guide trilogy, which was five books. Yeah, like that, seven are the new hopes, which is now even more confusing, because it's Episode Four, six is a Star Wars story Rogue One, five is a Star Wars story that is Solo, four is the revenge of the Sith, which is confusing, I know, because it's Episode Three, three are the wars of the clone, two are the attacks of the clones, one is the phantom menace in the cloud cities and the ground.

Who knows eleven? I know eleven: eleven is the last of the Jewdi. Actually, she's on Stranger Things, isn't she?, ten are the awakenings of the Force. Man, could you imagine if I included the TV series' too?, nine are the returns of the Jewdi, and we'll be three numbers off until the end, eight are the empires striking back, even though this is Episode Five. You know what this is like? The Hitchhikers Guide trilogy, which was five books. Yeah, like that, seven are the new hopes, which is now even more confusing, because it's Episode Four, six is a Star Wars story Rogue One, five is a Star Wars story that is Solo, four is the revenge of the Sith, which is confusing, I know, because it's Episode Three, three are the wars of the clone, two are the attacks of the clones, one is the phantom menace in the cloud cities and the ground.

שְׁנֵים עָשָׂר מִי יוֹדֵעַ? שְׁנֵים עָשָׂר אֲנִי יוֹדֵעַ:
שְׁנֵים עָשָׂר שִׁבְטַיָּא, אַחַד עָשָׂר כּוֹכְבַיָּא,
עֲשָׂרָה דִבְּרַיָּא, תִּשְׁעָה יַרְחֵי לֵדָה, שְׁמוֹנָה
יְמֵי מִילָה, שִׁבְעָה יְמֵי שַׁבַּתָּא, שִׁשָּׁה סִדְרֵי
מִשְׁנָה, חֲמִשָּׁה חוּמְשֵׁי תוֹרָה, אַרְבַּע
אִמָּהוֹת, שְׁלֹשָׁה אָבוֹת, שְׁנֵי לֻחוֹת הַבְּרִית,
אֶחָד אֱלֹהֵינוּ שֶׁבַּשָּׁמַיִם וּבָאָרֶץ.

שְׁלֹשָׁה עָשָׂר מִי יוֹדֵעַ? שְׁלֹשָׁה עָשָׂר אֲנִי
יוֹדֵעַ: שְׁלֹשָׁה עָשָׂר מִדַּיָּא. שְׁנֵים עָשָׂר
שִׁבְטַיָּא, אַחַד עָשָׂר כּוֹכְבַיָּא, עֲשָׂרָה
דִבְּרַיָּא, תִּשְׁעָה יַרְחֵי לֵדָה, שְׁמוֹנָה יְמֵי
מִילָה, שִׁבְעָה יְמֵי שַׁבַּתָּא, שִׁשָּׁה סִדְרֵי
מִשְׁנָה, חֲמִשָּׁה חוּמְשֵׁי תוֹרָה, אַרְבַּע
אִמָּהוֹת, שְׁלֹשָׁה אָבוֹת, שְׁנֵי לֻחוֹת הַבְּרִית,
אֶחָד אֱלֹהֵינוּ שֶׁבַּשָּׁמַיִם וּבָאָרֶץ.

Who knows twelve? I know twelve: twelve are the rises of Skywalker. Hey, maybe I should include the TV series'? Just kidding, eleven is the last of the Jewdi. Actually, she's on Stranger Things, isn't she?, ten are the awakenings of the Force. Man, could you imagine if I included the TV series' too?, nine are the returns of the Jewdi, and we'll be three numbers off until the end, eight are the empires striking back, even though this is Episode Five. You know what this is like? The Hitchhikers Guide trilogy, which was five books. Yeah, like that, seven are the new hopes, which is now even more confusing, because it's Episode Four, six is a Star Wars story Rogue One, five is a Star Wars story that is Solo, four is the revenge of the Sith, which is confusing, I know, because it's Episode Three, three are the wars of the clone, two are the attacks of the clones, one is the phantom menace in the cloud cities and the ground.

Who knows thirteen? I don't know thirteen, at least until they make another movie, in which case, this Haggadah will be dated, twelve are the rises of Skywalker. Hey, maybe I should include the TV series'? Just kidding, eleven is the last of the Jewdi. Actually, she's on Stranger Things, isn't she?, ten are the awakenings of the Force. Man, could you imagine if I included the TV series' too?, nine are the returns of the Jewdi, and we'll be three numbers off until the end, eight are the empires striking back, even though this is Episode Five. You know what this is like? The Hitchhikers Guide trilogy, which was five books. Yeah, like that, seven are the new hopes, which is now even more confusing, because it's Episode Four, six is a Star Wars story Rogue One, five is a Star Wars story that is Solo, four is the revenge of the Sith, which is confusing, I know, because it's Episode Three, three are the wars of the clone, two are the attacks of the clones, one is the phantom menace in the cloud cities and the ground.

חַד גַּדְיָא

חַד גַּדְיָא, חַד גַּדְיָא דְּזַבִּין אַבָּא בִּתְרֵי זוּזֵי, חַד
גַּדְיָא, חַד גַּדְיָא.

וְאָתָא שׁוּנְרָא וְאָכְלָה לְגַדְיָא, דְּזַבִּין אַבָּא בִּתְרֵי
זוּזֵי. חַד גַּדְיָא, חַד גַּדְיָא.

וְאָתָא כַלְבָּא וְנָשַׁךְ לְשׁוּנְרָא, דְּאָכְלָה לְגַדְיָא, דְּזַבִּין
אַבָּא בִּתְרֵי זוּזֵי. חַד גַּדְיָא, חַד גַּדְיָא.

וְאָתָא חוּטְרָא וְהִכָּה לְכַלְבָּא, דְּנָשַׁךְ לְשׁוּנְרָא,
דְּאָכְלָה לְגַדְיָא, דְּזַבִּין אַבָּא בִּתְרֵי זוּזֵי. חַד גַּדְיָא,
חַד גַּדְיָא.

וְאָתָא נוּרָא וְשָׂרַף לְחוּטְרָא, דְּהִכָּה לְכַלְבָּא, דְּנָשַׁךְ
לְשׁוּנְרָא, דְּאָכְלָה לְגַדְיָא, דְּזַבִּין אַבָּא בִּתְרֵי זוּזֵי.
חַד גַּדְיָא, חַד גַּדְיָא.

וְאָתָא מַיָּא וְכָבָה לְנוּרָא, דְּשָׂרַף לְחוּטְרָא, דְּהִכָּה
לְכַלְבָּא, דְּנָשַׁךְ לְשׁוּנְרָא, דְּאָכְלָה לְגַדְיָא, דְּזַבִּין
אַבָּא בִּתְרֵי זוּזֵי. חַד גַּדְיָא, חַד גַּדְיָא.

One Droid

One droid, one droid, that my father bought for two credits, one droid, one droid.

Then came a tooka and ate the droid, that my father bought for two credits, one droid, one droid.

Then came a massiff and bit the tooka, that ate the droid, that my father bought for two credits, one droid, one droid.

Then came a gaderffii and hit the massiff, that bit the tooka, that ate the droid, that my father bought for two credits, one droid, one droid.

Then came Mustafar lava and burnt the gaderffii, that hit the massiff, that bit the tooka, that ate the droid, that my father bought for two credits, one droid, one droid.

Then came farmed moisture and extinguished the Mustafar lava, that burnt the gaderffii, that hit the massiff, that bit the tooka, that ate the droid, that my father bought for two credits, one droid, one droid.

וְאָתָא תוֹרָא וְשָׁתָה לְמַיָּא, דְּכָבָה לְנוּרָא, דְּשָׂרַף
לְחוּטְרָא, דְּהִכָּה לְכַלְבָּא, דְּנָשַׁךְ לְשׁוּנְרָא, דְּאָכְלָה
לְגַדְיָא, דְּזַבִּין אַבָּא בִּתְרֵי זוּזֵי. חַד גַּדְיָא, חַד גַּדְיָא.

וְאָתָא הַשּׁוֹחֵט וְשָׁחַט לְתוֹרָא, דְּשָׁתָה לְמַיָּא, דְּכָבָה
לְנוּרָא, דְּשָׂרַף לְחוּטְרָא, דְּהִכָּה לְכַלְבָּא, דְּנָשַׁךְ
לְשׁוּנְרָא, דְּאָכְלָה לְגַדְיָא, דְּזַבִּין אַבָּא בִּתְרֵי זוּזֵי.
חַד גַּדְיָא, חַד גַּדְיָא.

וְאָתָא מַלְאַךְ הַמָּוֶת וְשָׁחַט לְשׁוֹחֵט, דְּשָׁחַט לְתוֹרָא,
דְּשָׁתָה לְמַיָּא, דְּכָבָה לְנוּרָא, דְּשָׂרַף לְחוּטְרָא,
דְּהִכָּה לְכַלְבָּא, דְּנָשַׁךְ לְשׁוּנְרָא, דְּאָכְלָה לְגַדְיָא,
דְּזַבִּין אַבָּא בִּתְרֵי זוּזֵי. חַד גַּדְיָא, חַד גַּדְיָא.

וְאָתָא הַקָּדוֹשׁ בָּרוּךְ הוּא וְשָׁחַט לְמַלְאַךְ הַמָּוֶת,
דְּשָׁחַט לְשׁוֹחֵט, דְּשָׁחַט לְתוֹרָא, דְּשָׁתָה לְמַיָּא,
דְּכָבָה לְנוּרָא, דְּשָׂרַף לְחוּטְרָא, דְּהִכָּה לְכַלְבָּא,
דְּנָשַׁךְ לְשׁוּנְרָא, דְּאָכְלָה לְגַדְיָא, דְּזַבִּין אַבָּא בִּתְרֵי
זוּזֵי. חַד גַּדְיָא, חַד גַּדְיָא.

Then came a rancor and drank the farmed moisture, that extinguished the Mustafar lava, that burnt the gaderffii, that hit the massiff, that bit the tooka, that ate the droid, that my father bought for two credits, one droid, one droid.

Then came the beastmaster and slaughtered the rancor, that drank the farmed moisture, that extinguished the Mustafar lava, that burnt the gaderffii, that hit the massiff, that bit the tooka, that ate the droid, that my father bought for two credits, one droid, one droid.

Then came the Emperor of death and slew the beastmaster, who slaughtered the rancor, that drank the farmed moisture, that extinguished the Mustafar lava, that burnt the gaderffii, that hit the massiff, that bit the tooka, that ate the droid, that my father bought for two credits, one droid, one droid.

Then came the Chosen One, blessed be She and smote the Emperor of death, who slew the beastmaster, who slaughtered the rancor, that drank the farmed moisture, that extinguished the Mustafar lava, that burnt the gaderffii, that hit the massiff, that bit the tooka, that ate the droid, that my father bought for two credits, one droid, one droid.

About Marbo Mabro[*]

Martin Bodek was born and raised in Brooklyn, New York. He currently lives in New Jersey with his wife and three children. He is an avid marathoner, Daf Yomi participant, Wordler, vexillologist, and halvah aficionado. He is a technologist by day, and a writer by night.

He has been writing freelance for over two decades, mostly on Jewish interest topics. He is the co-creator of a popular Jewish news satire website called TheKnish.com. His work has been published in *The Huffington Post, The Denver Post, The Washington Times, The Jewish Press, Country Yossi Magazine, Modern Magazine, The Jewish Link of NJ*, The Jewish Book Council, bangitout.com, scoogiespin.com, jewcentral.com, and israelinsider.com. His work has also been translated for Germany's only weekly Jewish newspaper, *The Jüdische Allgemeine*. He has served as the beat reporter for JRunnersClub.org and as the surname columnist for jewishworldreview.com.

The Emoji Haggadah, The Festivus Haggadah, The Coronavirus Haggadah, and *The Shakespeare Haggadah* generated much praise and media attention, and were covered in *The Jewish Week, The Jewish Link of NJ, Jewish Vues*, Vos Iz Neias, Jewish Book Council, NorthJersey.com, *The Forward*, Jewish Journal, J-Wire, Vox, *The Jewish Press*, The Jewish Fund, *The Jerusalem Post*, The Jewish Telegraphic Agency, *The Jüdische Allgemeine*, Moked, various blogs, eater.com, nj1015.com, New York Shakespeare Instagram Live, The Cindy Grosz Show, and The New York Times.

Zaidy's War, the memoir of his grandfather's unreal WWII experience, launched Martin on an international, multi-venue public speaking/podcast/Zoom talk/book club tour that remains ongoing.

This Haggadah is the Way is his twelfth book. He'll eat it up, he loves it so.

---

[*] Create your own Star Wars name! Forename: combine the first three letters of your forename and the first two of your surname. Surname: combine the first two letters of your mother's maiden name and the first three of your birth city.

The Circle is Now Complete